# MIXED
# ☐ EMOTIONS

SUNY Series in the Sociology of Emotions

Theodore D. Kemper, Editor

# MIXED EMOTIONS

## Certain Steps
## Toward Understanding Ambivalence

Andrew J. Weigert

*State University of New York Press*

Published by
State University of New York Press, Albany

For information, address State University of New York
Press, State University Plaza, Albany, N.Y., 12246

Production by Diane Ganeles
Marketing by Theresa A. Swierzowski

**Library of Congress Cataloging-in-Publication Data**

Weigert, Andrew J.
    Mixed emotions : certain steps toward understanding ambivalence /
Andrew J. Weigert.
        p.   cm.  —(SUNY series in the sociology of emotions)
    Includes bibliographical references  (p.   ) and index.
    ISBN 0–7914-0600–8 (Ch. : acid-free) . —ISBN 0–7914-0601–6 (Pb.  :
acid-free)
    1. Ambivalence. 2. Ambivalence—Social aspects. 3. Civilization,
Modern—20th century—Psychological aspects.  4. Social psychology.
I. Title. II. Series.
BF575.A45W45   1991
302.5'4—dc20                                                    90–9888
                                                                    CIP

10 9 8 7 6 5 4 3 2 1

To Kathleen
    Karen and Sheila

Who show how marital
        and parental

Ambivalences end

    finally

In love

# Contents

# List of Figures and Tables

# Acknowledgments

Permission to reproduce slightly revised versions of the following materials is gratefully acknowledged:

"Ambivalence: A Touchstone of the Modern Temper," pp. 205–227 in David D. Franks and E. Doyle McCarthy (eds.), The Sociology of Emotions, Greenwich: JAI Press, 1989; and "Joyful Disaster," pp. 73–88 in Volume 50, No. 1, Sociological Analysis.

Much appreciated help in typing and preparing the manuscript came from the Faculty Word Processing Center of the University of Notre Dame, especially Nancy Kegler, Cheryl Reed, and Sherry Reichold. Much is owed to conversations over two decades with fellow ex-graduate students who suffered my ambivalent responses: David Franks, Viktor Gecas, Mark Hutter, Elizabeth Rooney, and Darwin Thomas. Finally, I thank my family, Kathleen, Karen, and Sheila, to whom this book is dedicated unambivalently.

# Introduction

This book is a piece of autobiographical genre: trying to make sense of one's life with sociological tools. I came to sociology via one of the best Western traditions of reason and faith, the Jesuits, and after living in a society pulled between two cultures, Puerto Rico. Returning to the Mainland and leaving the Jesuits, perhaps it is no wonder that one of the first topics I wrote about as a graduate student was ambivalence and the religious experience. This book presents twenty-five years of avocational follow up. Two intellectual developments brought the work to fruition: the writings of Robert Merton on structural ambivalence as characteristic of those paragons of modern life, the professions; and recent sociological perspectives on affective experience, the emotions.

The present essay is a synthetic exposition, an extended reflection. It uses ambivalence heuristically, as a "sensitizing concept" to stimulate theoretical elaboration and empirical investigation. Underlying the exposition are three arguments, each less defended than the next. The arguments, undefended here, have to be elaborated by others who may be drawn to do so if this book succeeds in eliciting the intended Aha! experience. The first undefended and largely unmentioned argument would be a philosophical anthropological thesis that the human animal is both suffi-

ciently structured and open enough to experience simultaneous pushes and pulls in a single field of action. A stronger
version of this argument would show that there are dualities in the human condition that focus the structured open-
ness more or less dichotomously. The second undefended
but suggested argument is a socio-historical one contained,
among other places, in the perspective of conventional
sociological thought, namely, that society has become
increasingly pluralistic and complex. I would add: and its
dwellers increasingly ambivalent. Usual analyses of modern
life reiterate institutional, communicative, and cognitive
pluralism, but they leave largely unaddressed the possibility of emotional pluralism. A stronger version of this argument could be based functionally on the first, were it posited for the sake of argument. It would go like this: since
humans are essentially ambivalent, an inefficient and
painful condition, a primary and traditional function of culture is to resolve ambivalence and allow the pursuit of an
orderly and contented life. A secondary issue arises: is modern society also less able to resolve ambivalence?

A weaker version of the argument drops philosophical
anthropological talk and states that ambivalence, if any is
documented, is generated by sets of historical institutions
and cultural imperatives, and adequately resolved by other
sets of institutional arrangements. The third undefended
but explicitly urged argument derives from this weaker version. It says simply that modern life is characterized by contradictory structures, imperatives, and experiences for
which today's culture has weak, if any, resolutions. The
modern person must undergo ambivalence cold turkey, as it
were. This statement touches the main and modest goal of
the book: to indicate experiences and situations in which
ambivalence is likely to be felt, and to bring together illus-
trative writings about such happenings.

If the indications and illustrations are successful, then
there is a body of presumptive social facts that call for
attention. The empirically discovered, though theory
informed facts drive a quest for deeper understanding. Furthermore, contradictory situations and experiences can

now be interpreted through a conceptual object constructed at the turn of the century. Experiences now labeled and
known as ambivalent may always have been felt, but they
were psyche-soma, matter-form, body-soul, mind-body, rea-
son-feeling, pity-fear, God's grace-Devil's temptation, altru-
ism-egotism, duty-selfishness. With our modern construct,
we can realize these experiences as ambivalence, and really
feel modern. Indeed, the experience, to be made real and
known as real, can be grasped as ambivalence, an historical
first. Only our era has ambivalence as an objective reality
formed, labeled, and lived in responses to contradictory
aspects of situations.

   With these arguments simmering in the text, I present,
first, general aspects of the social condition of human animals with an eye on the contemporary scene. Then follows
a sketch of a sociology of emotions as the theoretical
framework for the discussion. Next, I look at the central
concept of a sociological psychology, the self. This scrutiny
is informally organized around the phenomenological
aspects of: individual, appearances, time, space, and imagined future. Then aspects of social reality are considered:
collective life and dominant institutional arrangements
such as family, work, school, leisure, and self-inclusion or
exclusion. The next theme brings us back to the seminal
topic, ambivalence and religion. The discussion is organized around the sacred, institutional dilemmas, and
absorption of the meaning of nuclear holocaust through
religious eschatological thinking. The last chapter recapitu-
lates and adds theoretical punch by reflecting on ambivalence toward consumerism as the human animal uses up
the earth it walks upon.[1]

---

1. John P. Hewitt's book, *Dilemmas of the American Self* (Temple University Press, 1989), came too late into my hands. It develops supportive arguments through a social psychological analysis of tensions within American society.

# Chapter 1

□

# Certain Opening Words

"We just have to take what comes." "Who knows God's will?" "The data are insufficient to solve the problem." "There are many sides to the issue." "Reasonable people do not agree on the facts." "We don't know what the outcome will be." Each of these assertions makes immediate sense to a modern person. As long as we are awake, we need to do something. Occasionally, the audacious uncertainty of what it means to do something breaks through the crust of custom and habit: we need some sense of what the future will be or what our actions will bring in order to go on doing what we are about. Uncertainties are a central component of the modern search for meaning (see Wuthnow 1988).

In the face of the uncertainties projected above, we have countervailing accounts that allow us to act decisively, with a sense that we know what we are doing, even though the *what* has not yet happened. Equally emphatic accounts can be called upon to assert a certain definition of the situation and motivate a course of action. After all, "Fate decrees," "God wills," "Father knows best," "Rationality demands," and "The data dictate"—and I am sure of that. Each account appeals to us when the situation demands.

Analysts attribute the first set of accounts to a world of change, variety, complexity, empiricism, and rationality; that is, to what is generally taken as modern society, charac-

1

terized by heightened uncertainty. We sharpen what we mean by modern through comparisons with other types of society, such as one in which the second set of accounts that pre-empt uncertainty would make sense.

The genre of this book is that of an exploratory essay in the form of a wheel with a central idea from which radiate substantive developments. Interpretive punch is gained from a running, though speculative, thought experiment that implicitly compares contemporary society with other types of societies. Much of the comparison is based on the conventional contrasts that underlay the emergence of sociology: the transition from what we generically think of as traditional society to our present situation that many struggle to christen as modern. A similar running contrast informs this discussion with focus on its implications for making sense out of affective experiences that simultaneously attract and repel from a course of action analogous to contradictory cognitive renditions of that action. If the reader prefers the essay as such, the implicit comparisons generated by the thought experiment can simply be tuned out. Be forewarned, however, that they warrant the line of development in the text, since I am convinced that even an implicit and heuristic sense of historical comparison is better than none at all.

An underlying theme is that the relevance and plausibility of accounts follows from the kind of society in which we live. Without attempting a comparative historical analysis, fairly conventional types of society serve as implicit comparisons to make sense out of the contemporary situation. The types are heuristic only; their purpose is to provide a hypothetical comparative context for the discussion of ambivalence as a modern form of life.

### Heuristic Types of Societies

There have been traditional types of societies that were smaller, slower changing, more group conscious, and orally oriented to myth and dicta. These societies had traditional empowered sources of answers to the issues of self-understanding, social rules, relationship to nature, and paths of proper action. Members of traditional societies can be said to know who they were; how they should relate to others and to the physical world; and what they should do. In other words, there were known legitimate sources of answers to the questions that arise in everyone's narrative of self-understanding, or sense of biography. Centrally organized around a kinship structure of blood or symbolic relationships, short-lived individuals found a world of real meanings that defined them, others, and the environment from birth to an early death, probably in their thirties. Subsistence was the order of the day. Significant changes within an individual's lifetime were likely to be sudden and catastrophic, whether from famine, conquest, or another of the Four Horsemen. Social time moves slowly; recent change bursts on the scene like a stranger from another world. Society's stories were recounted in epics and tragedies telling of an objective world of Fate, Gods and Heros. Epic and dramatic art taught cautionary tales about each person's known and ascribed place in a scheme devised by nature's gods (cf. Baumeister 1986; Bellah,1964; Berger 1967).

A second type pictures a society organized along lines of production hierarchies, from feudal and rural to urban and proletarian. Modern production-oriented societies reach out to imperialist or transnational relationships. Societies produce surpluses of specialized goods to support specialized occupational and social groups arranged in increasingly complex status ladders of privilege, power, and wealth heaped at the top. For those at the bottom of the ladders, life's meanings remain relatively restraining. Legitimation of social arrangements is anchored in traditional religiously based beliefs about how the world worked, and even more powerfully, how it should work. For emerging middle classes, however, internal sources of change such as arts, crafts, and the powerful technological impact of science fueled new ways of thinking and living. With external exploration and imperialist conquest, new production and marketing possibilities ushered in an urban cosmopolitan world legitimating bourgeois reformulations of traditional ways of life. Inherited objective, collective, and oral meanings were transformed into subjective, individualistic, and discursive counter accounts of how the world works. The novel is crafted to tell the stories of beknighted lives. Individuals, not clans, must find the good life within new forms of social organization that make individual good a supreme cultural value (cf. Weber 1958).

Today's societies present a third type of organization. Modern institutions are structured into bureaucracies peopled by service workers in white shirts or pink blouses. Status and opportunity come from educational entre into preferred professional, executive, and hi-tech careers. High entry-level salaries make increasing consumption of technological gadgetry into the status game par excellence for those with diploma certification. Interlocking media driven by silicon chips and laser beams make expanding computer, video, and telecommunication into a kind of super-organic mind. The environment is transformed into overlapping sets of media images and ever-expanding markets. Without a unified comprehension of events, meanings are overlaid, fragmented, changing, and relativistic. Answers are sought pell-mell. Discarded and primitive inspirations, now vaguely free of content, are revived for psychological closure and therapeutic consolation. Ancient wisdom becomes a series of cliches; that is, sayings used for feeling good rather than thinking clearly or believing firmly (Zidjerveld 1979). Serious searchers after religious truth, for example, are forced to be heretics who must choose among warring creeds, each made implausible by the strength of the others in a pluralistic world (Berger 1980). Multi-media re-presentations of the world are crafted on video or film, with the story line sacrificed for the imagery. Stories, like life, have no dramatic unity with a beginning, middle, and end; they merely start, stop, and re-run.

The mediated "information" society has no unquestioned idea about beginnings and endings, not even concerning human life: witness the abortion bitterness and the pulling-the-plug debates. Framing the debates is the specter of possible nuclear holocaust or ecological disaster that would end life's stories as we know them. Cosmologists' theories of the "big bang" origins of the world are matched with the mirror imagery of the big bang of nuclear exchange that may slow life-support systems with a big chill freezing mammals in their dens.

## Modernity: Pluralism and Multivalence

These types of societal organization are mingled in our lives from lingering enchanted beliefs about magical fulfillment to the humming VCR recording simultaneous transmission of world events. Persons living in the centers of modern societies have a consciousness shaped by the pressures of pluralism. Analysts of different persuasions agree that today's societies are characterized by increasingly formal, specialized, and differentiated institutions, the key organizational features of modern life. Consider such indicators as: the ubiquity of bureaucracy; the centralization of large-scale government; the spread of legal definitions of actions and relationships; the increase of high technology thinking and instruments; and the growth of world-wide markets based on specialized knowledge and technologies. In a word, the cosmos is transformed from a universe to a multiverse, from isolated states into an international village in which everyone is a possible neighbor or victim of someone else's conflict. Modernity is characterized by the depth and pervasiveness of the "dilemmatic" attitude; namely, structural contradictions built into societal organization that result in cognitive dilemmas at the common sense and ideological levels (Billig et al. 1988).

Many would so describe today's world. What is rarely seen, however, is the affective or emotional counterpart to the segmented structures of society. Social organization shapes the organization of self understanding *and* self-feeling (see Franks and McCarthy 1989). Persons who see the world as a *universe* live in plausibility structures that make univalent feelings meaningful (cf. Berger 1967). This is not to say that such persons live a monotone life. Rather, the point is that such social organization includes affective organization as well, e.g., there would be feeling rules and a mundane theory of emotions that render an emotion real *in situ,* by contrast with modern pluralism. Persons whose world hangs together have a chance to experience feelings that make sense as well. Persons born into a slow-changing traditional society based on clear kinship roles with author-itative cultural rules and shared religious rituals know what to feel; how to define it; how to display it; and to whom.

On the other hand, persons positioned in a *multi*verse of intersecting circles of roles and rituals are faced with the psychic engineering task of arranging feelings into a mean-ingful whole. If many meanings are plausible, many feelings are meaningful. And the meanings may not be the same that our parents felt. Furthermore, according to the comparative logic of social life, the co-existence of plausible meanings renders each less plausible in some proportion to the plau-sibility of each. The low plausibility of the flat earth society does little to shake belief in a round earth, whereas the high plausibility of American nationalism threatens belief in the plausibility of world citizenship. The multivalent modern faces a characteristically modern dilemma: the ambiguity of competing meanings and the ambivalence of conflicting feelings.

Institutions that render different worldviews plausible underwrite conflicting emotional experiences. A member of a traditional society would be likely to experience life in the rather univalent emotional tone consistent with the defini-tions structured into each situation. A person was born into a station in life and progressed through a series of statuses on the way to death at an age which today is tragically young.

A contemporary, however, is likely to find any situation a complex of possible meanings with different plausibilities associated with, not just many, but contradictory emotional meanings. Carriers of modern culture are "multivalent" per-sons with no certain answers to questions about personal authenticity (cf. Lee 1966; Trilling 1972). Peter Berger finds modernity in the "transition from fate to choice" felt in a "highly ambivalent" way (1980: 20). Modernity is keyed to an ambivalent struggle between liberation and alienation, between individual freedom and group security, as in the Third World and Eastern Europe celebrating freedom even as traditional statuses and jobs are lost.

## Implications for the Individual

To the extent that the human animal is a relatively non-instinctual organism, social structures channel energy, guide action, and constitute meanings. This is the psychological relevance of social institutions; society shapes self. Social scientists speak of the second nature of habit, self-repeating internalized rules and norms, or social personality that makes individuals into enculturated persons (cf. Young 1988). Within larger social arrangements,we speak of the "institutionalization" of the human organism (Berger and Luckmann 1966).

As institutionalized, an individual acquires a pragmatic self that enables it to act meaningfully. A self knows how to perform as a reasonably competent male or female, black or white, rich or poor actor within whatever circumstances of identity are relevant here and now (Weigert et al. 1986). The options are culturally organized into hierarchies, both internal and external, that shape one's biography (Stryker 1980). From an objective perspective, these forces may be real or fictive, determined or voluntary, rational or irrational, but to the individual, they are situational demands within which he or she must act here and now. There is no escaping the need to act or to decide not to act. Society functions within and without as a real force transforming the multivalence of the "pre-social individual" into the mundane valences that make the organism a human person, a competent member of the group. Typically, it appears that competent members knew who they were and what they felt, or they knew how to find out. Emotional lives were channeled within mundane and unquestioned force lines. A normal self was part of a collective self with no need of emotional police. A modern self, by contrast, is adrift in unchartered seas.

This simplified typology of modern life is the background for the recent sociological psychological analysis of emotions. A central thesis is that society transforms the assumed multivalence of animals born to human parents into predictable and meaningful emotions (e.g., McCarthy 1989). There is no agreement on the mechanism that transforms animal feelings into human emotions. Possible explanations include physiological processes, psychoanalytic dynamics, structured relations, rules of interaction, cultural maps, or abstract cognitive schema. All agree that emotions are problematic in the modern world. These explanations try to fill a gap: how do we understand emotional life in a world in which feelings and sensibility can no longer be taken for granted?

Emotional experience cannot be understood simply as good and evil forces, of God's grace and the Devil's temptations. Nor are emotions morally neutral surges following natural laws of physiology or neurochemistry. Religious transformations and scientific reductions do not offer total explanations of emotions. Emotional life needs to be meaningful, and meanings are socially constructed and interactionally realized. Analysis must include socially available definitions and interpretations of emotional experience.

An axiom of the sociology of knowledge states that new ideas arise to explain previously taken-for-granted experience, and signal the plausibility of an alternative worldview and the relevance of a new interpretive focus. Such a signal was given with the coining and currency of the concept "ambivalence" within the psychoanalytic movement at the dawn of the twentieth century. It found its way also into sociological analysis (see Merton 1976). Psychoanalysis and sociology point to aspects of modernity that need attention. Our concern is with the sociological payoff.

Up to now I have presented general perspectives on social organization and self-understanding. Focus now centers on an emotional issue; namely, making sense out of ambivalence as a characteristic of modern sensibility.

Before facing the task, consider a sociological psychological framework that deepens our understanding of emotions.

## *Outline of a Sociological Psychology of Emotions*

In the last decade, scholars laid the foundations for a sociological psychology of emotions (Denzin 1984; Finkelstein 1980; Franks and McCarthy 1989; Gordon 1981; Harré 1986; Hochschild 1975; 1983; Kemper 1978; Shott 1979). Their work enables us to understand emotions as links between social organization and the way we interpret experience. Specific discussion of ambivalence from a broad social constructionist perspective follows in the next chapter.

As a species of animal, it appears likely that there are universal feeling responses that humans signal through bodily gestures, especially facial expression (Ekman and Friesen 1975). Some feelings seem to be structured into the autonomic nervous system. These feelings are then culturally defined and transformed into socially meaningful emotions. Gestural expression of feelings has been functional in human evolution. Indeed, analogous gestures in other animals are interpretable anthropomorphically from Fido's presumably happily wagging tail to the chimpanzee's presumably happy smile. Humans normally lack tails, but we smile. We presumably know what the smiler means or is feeling—but we are not sure. The smile may mean: a seductive come-on; an embarrassing faux pas; a thinly masked sense of outrage; or a shrug of cosmic irony at human silliness.

Even granting possibly universal emotional gestures, the arena for a sociology of emotions covers the interpretative link between the behavioral display of feelings and what the displayer is experiencing, and that between what the display means to the displayer and to the audiences. If there are no fixed links among feelings, behaviors, and the meanings that self and others attach to them, then we must examine the ways in which those meanings and links are socially constructed. Physiological and neurological components of feelings are real and measurable, but they are pre-social, as yet without social meaning and thus not yet the subject of a sociological interpretation of emotions.

Social analysis of emotions starts with the "self-feeling" of the person (Denzin 1984). Self-feelings refer to immediate and concrete private experiences each of us has of a flow of affect, mood, or sensibilities. We experience a triple awareness: feelings; self-experiencing the feelings; and our revealing or masking of the feelings. The flow of inner experiences is the bedrock of personal emotions. Self and other interpret the gestural and verbal concomitants of self-feelings within social processes that link self, situation, and the larger socio-political order, just as a child learns to link its wailing with parental responses.

Self-feelings are a phenomenological base for authentic experience of self and meaningful interaction with others. They do not, however, provide the rules for channeling or interpreting action appropriate to the situation (Hochschild 1975). Culture provides rules defining which feelings are typical for a normal person here and now. Routinely competent action results from a complicated confluence of acquired definitions governing self-feelings linked with gestural responses and cultural rules. The person experiences this confluence and routinely labels it so that self can understand the phenomenological flow of feelings and align them with actions that others accept as normal. Failure to interpret the confluence creates personal doubt about one's morality or sanity, and failure to act in accord with public definitions of what one should be feeling can lead to the imposition of a criminal or insane identity.

Anthropologists show how different cultures know the world differently through language reflecting social structure and perceived environments. So too, persons divide up and interpret their feelings according to cultural categories (e.g. White & Kirkpatrick 1985). They learn a "vocabulary of emotions" (Geertz 1959) that supplies the definitions and words for transforming raw bodily feelings into appropriately defined self-feelings, that is, for transforming organic changes into socially meaningful emotions leading to appropriate action.

For our purposes, an emotion is a *socially defined feeling* (Weigert 1983; cf. the "emotionology" of Stearns and Stearns 1986; and the social construction of emotions, e.g., Franks and McCarthy 1989; Harré 1986). As socially defined feelings, emotions are meaningful symbolic transformations of the flow of raw experience. They are personal and social sentient meanings that involve the body as constitutive oᶠ the affective meaning (cf. Scheff 1983). By contrast, the voice or gestures that we use to construct and communicate ideas are in principle detachable from the meanings that the symbols carry. The mere body can be considered a neutral medium for the literal semantic meaning of the cognitive symbol qua cognitive, just as the black and white of the printed page are detachable from the meanings of the sentences they carry. Taken by themselves, the black and white marks carry no other meaning than the lexicographical definitions of the words they form. Theirs are the literal meanings found in a dictionary. Even if typed to communicate emotions, printed words do so without feeling.

The embodied person, on the other hand, sentiently constitutes emotions, since self feels or thinks as well as displays or feigns them. The body can be interpreted as communicating feelings through the array of expressions that it "gives off" whenever it gives any expression at all (Goffman 1959). Through unavoidably apparent symbols like voice qualities, facial gestures, mien and gate, stance and distancing, the person necessarily displays emotional meanings, whether or not they are intended or even felt. It is never certain how much of the display is intended, controlled, known to the self, or perceived by the other. The displayer may be feigning, gesturally incompetent, or simply densely unaware—as the other may be as well. These inherent interactional uncertainties add spice to relationships in which emotional communication is central, as in courtship, seduction, spying, or parenting. Modern relationships, presumably premised on accurate understanding of each other's subjectivity amidst increasingly slippery symbols, must be forged on such uncertainties. They become grist for the therapeutic mill.

Assuming that self knows *how* to display emotions competently, there are additional cultural rules governing when the emotions are appropriate and the gestural variations that ought to be displayed. Joy upon meeting a married friend of the opposite sex is displayed appropriately with a rather tight-lipped kiss on the cheek or into the air as cheek touches cheek, but never by an open-mouthed kiss of lips upon lips. Even supposedly irresistible imperatives of physical pain follow cultural rules governing who experiences how much pain, when and how it is displayed, and to whom (Zborowski 1969).

Political rules guide who may express which emotion toward whom (Hochschild,1975). Such rules highlight interactional politics because they follow power and subordination. A secretary, for example, may not without risk display public anger toward the boss, whereas the boss may without risk of ceasing to be boss display anger against the secretary. The same goes for the sergeant toward corporals; parents toward children, and teachers toward pupils (cf. Stearns and Stearns 1986). Yet, in contemporary America there is ambivalence toward anger itself. Carol Tavris states that "ambivalence about anger permeates our society" (1982: 26). American response to the feeling defined as anger has changed historically and currently elicits mixed feelings. Tavris traces a line of thought that posits a traditional attitude based on the belief that we can and typically ought to control anger. The revolution in understanding human nature contained in Darwinian and Freudian views, however, implied that, in the final analysis, we cannot control anger. Finally, there is a modern attitude emerging that, we ought not control it. Anger can be seen as sinful or as self-fulfillment. Mixed feelings in anger-inducing situations echo mixed historical and attitudinal messages. Even anger lingers ambivalently.

In general, positive emotions are displayed up the status ladder, and negative emotions are likely to flow down the ladder. It truly feels tougher at the bottom, and one is not even allowed to display these feelings openly. Personal feelings are socially elicited and defined according to one's position in the organization of status and power. Being male or female, black or white, doctor or janitor, carries with it different emotional lives that flow from social structures not from genes or hormones. Being shapes feeling as well as having and doing. Social scientists note that females traditionally give support and love while males seek worldly status and recognition. Women pursue occupations involving positive emotional labor while men are allowed to display negative emotions in a wider variety of occupations (cf. Hochschild 1983). These social paths are associated with different emotional lives; we are taught what to feel and how to define and display what we feel. In the process, we construct our feeling selves along certain career and life lines.

Enacting internalized emotional rules, individuals interpret their feelings as socially meaningful; experience them as motives for action; and construct a sense of self as sincere, authentic, or possessed of whatever moral tone is validated here and now (Trilling 1972). Situationally appropriate, aptly displayed feelings reenforce and reproduce the structural arrangements of society. Typically, actors feel internally what the external structure defines as legitimate (see Shott 1979). Cultural values link feelings with a moral universe within which my self makes sense. I feel, therefore I am. I feel righteous, therefore I am righteous. I feel saved, therefore I am saved.

No system works perfectly, however. Indeed, modern society, as we saw above, is characterized by pluralism, ambiguity, and uncertainty. Contradictory rules sometimes cover a single situation. In today's world there are often contradictory expectations attached to a single role, status, or situation that leads to "sociological ambivalence" (Merton 1976; Merton et al. 1983).

Contradictory expectations concern actions and feelings. Contradictory definitions of feelings make it difficult to experience self as a single emotional being. If I do not know what I am feeling, then I do not know who I am nor what to do. My identity is called into question. Why does the radiant bride feel fear and anxiety as well as joy as she walks down the aisle to marry the man she thinks she knows, and whose "wife" she wants to be? Why does the filial son feel relief and guilt as well as sorrow while he walks behind the coffin of his long-loved mother? In the former situation, there are two feeling rules governing the experience of the bride: rejoice and be wary. In the latter, there is one cultural rule: feel sorrow; but there may be a deeper dynamic that even culture cannot make explicitly legitimate: feel relief that the inevitable death has been survived at least for the time being; not to mention psychoanalytic interpretations about ambivalent Oedipal love toward a mother. No culture seems to have explicitly codified such ambivalence as legitimate or normative, though Susan Cole (1985) speculates that tragic form developed from mourning rituals designed to allay ambivalence toward the dead. Shoring up self's passage through these feeling crises are institutional arrangements that define experience, guide action, and prevent our deserting life at the last minute.

Cultural rules guiding emotional lives are linked with the structure of social relations. How we feel toward others, define and display those feelings, and direct our emotional lives are structured by the relationships of power and status. Power and status are universal components of social interaction and as such they enter into the dynamics of feelings and emotions. A person who experiences too much or too little power or status is likely to define the accompanying feeling in culturally consistent ways. Using too much power leads the user to feel guilt; receiving too much status makes the recipient feel shame. Having too little power, on the other hand, makes the impotent feel anxiety and fear; whereas receiving too little status leads the depreciated to feel depression or low self-esteem (Kemper 1978; and cf. Thomas et al. 1974).

Power and status link situational emotions with more inclusive emotions. Moderns, for example, may experience complexes of vague feelings about self mixed with attachments to ephemeral things and fleeting fads, in other words, materialistic narcissism (Lasch 1979). Other cultural complexes of feelings may be defined as patriotism, if they are experienced during flag waving on the Fourth of July; or nationalism, if the occasion is a military threat to the Nation; or Divine Presence, if the situation is one of religious ritual, personal tragedy, or millennial exaltation.

Complex emotions totalize the self, that is, they provide a single definition of various feelings that unifies the experiences in terms of a single transcendent symbol or idea. Such cultural emotions are socially constructed unifications of feelings that ground emotional life in meanings beyond the power of the individual as such. The totalized self gains emotional unification to the extent that the definition of the feeling complex is believed and embraced. Such unification and power creates a kind of motivational fusion that generates considerable energy in the service of those parties who carry the unifying symbols. Totalized selves are traditional products of religion's "sacred cosmos" (cf. Berger 1967). New converts dedicate their lives and fortunes to the sect; young recruits march to their deaths in defense of God's Nation; eschatological believers await the end of the world with joyful anticipation (Weigert 1988).

In summary, a sociological approach interprets emotions as socially constructed definitions of feelings that link body and situation in a system of meaning. These meanings are relatively independent of bureaucratic, technological, and formally rational meanings. This independence, or functional autonomy, makes possible an emotional lag that scholars have identified under various rubrics. The point is that emotional meaning is unable to keep pace with other systems of meanings: we are unable to emote appropriately about events generated by technology, biology, or reasons of state. How do you "feel" about terrorism, AIDS, nuclear war, or famine as you sit in your living room watching emaciated children starving or young men dying on evening TV?

Large-scale rationalities like technology, reasons of state, or international markets make some sense out of external forces and public events. Emotional rationality, however, must make sense out of the internal, private experience of those external events. Publically available symbols must be simultaneously meaningful to the inner life of the self if individuals are to feel integrated into the flow of

events. After elections, the winners and hopefully the losers
still feel politically integrated. At national holidays and collective rituals, all have a chance to feel integrated. There are
likely to be some, however, who reject emotional integration and others whom the power structure excludes. The
apathetic and oppressed do not live the public life.

Emotions are constitutive of self in a way that is irreducible to behavioral or cognitive links. Indeed, feelings
are deep signs of the way in which the organic self relates
to external events (Hochschild 1983). Defining these feelings as socially meaningful emotions symbolically transforms that deep link into objective cultural meanings.
Thus, personal inner feelings are engineered into publically
available motives and emotional meanings in a naturally
occurring world. Self becomes a competent displayer of
appropriate self-feelings in that world. Sensibilities do, at
times, integrate self and society. Integration is both an analytic and empirical issue. Let us attend first to one analytic
aspect and hope that others will see the need for empirical
work to follow.

### Mixed Emotions, Actions, and Ambiguity: The Temper of Feeling Our Times

Action, unless totally instinctual, robotic, or habitual,
requires decisiveness. The actor's plans for the long term;
motives influencing the actor in the situation; and objects
surrounding the actor must be interpreted and arranged
according to lines of relevance for the action at hand
(Schutz 1970). Although lines of relevance are typically
masked by the unquestioned routines of everyday life, we
know that things around us exist as already categorized
objects and potential motives. At one routine level of analysis, our circumstances bounce us around like stoppers on a
pin-ball machine. Alarm clocks make us go and red lights
make us stop. As motives, circumstances spark us into
action; otherwise, we merely bob around passively or
behave like drones in a hive. The active and passive path

each has its attraction. At times, we dip into passive reverie or plunge into mindless routine. Each can heal us for the moment, and we are emboldened to bear the next decision for acting anew.

We know what it means to be decisive. The actor must know the facts; interpret the causes and consequences likely to surround the facts; and act effectively to bring about the hoped-for results. Within the theater of the mind, or the logical world of mental experiments, the contemplating actor imagines events following the lawful dynamics of those imagined worlds. As ordered, they provide the cognitive basis for action, though the action may or may not be in line with real external forces.

Action halts, however, if the objects are so ambiguous that they cannot be categorized adequately for the actor's purpose. As Alfred Schutz illustrated, if that coiled thing in the corner looks equally like a rope or a snake, we cannot act on it until that ambiguity is settled. If more irrigation is likely both to increase food supplies and to cause serious soil degradation, then we cannot act with certainty. Once we know that the thing in the corner is a rope, then knowledge of ropes, gravity, and trees comes into play as we prepare to loop the rope around the hickory tree high enough to insure that when cut it will fall on the mark. Needless to say, we would have no ambiguity about trying to loop a snake around that hickory tree. Resolving ambiguity is a first step toward decisive action, but not the last.

Ambiguity, in contrast to ambivalence, refers to the cognitive domain; namely, a confusion or contest of ideas (cf. Zielyk 1966). It refers to a situation in which we do not know whether something is this or that, since it appears like each. Donald Levine (1985) has argued that a "flight from ambiguity" is characteristic of a modernity committed to clarity. Nevertheless, ambiguity remains with us. Levine argues that it is desirable for evoking complex meanings and constructing diffuse symbols of social life (1985: 218). Ambivalence, on the other hand, refers to the mixed feelings we have toward an object, such as attraction and repulsion at the same time. Experience commingles elements of cognitive and affective responses toward objects; yet reflection justifies the distinction between knowledge and emotion.

Faced with coiled ambiguity in a corner, we experience attraction and repulsion as we both feel drawn toward it to learn what it is, and feel an urge to flee out of fear of the unknown. This primitive ambivalence is felt in the presence of a "thing" before we have any warrant to be sure of what it is. Once we recognize what the thing is and securely categorize it, our ambivalence fades, at least for the time being. In our newfound sureness, we feel safe in handling the rope, or fearfully relieved as we silently leave the snake to its sleep.

The distinction between cognition and emotion becomes clearer in instances in which there is no ambiguity about the object. We definitely identify the thing as a nuclear bomb. It is a clearly known object. Yet, we may still feel repulsion and attraction toward it, as in Robert Oppenheimer's religious language on witnessing the first nuclear detonation, "I am become Death, the destroyer of worlds" (see Weart 1988: 101). We are fascinated by it even as we fear it. This is what we call object ambivalence: contradictory feelings elicited simultaneously by a single defined object. The object may be a person whose public identity is clear, but whose personal relationship to me is uncertain: I know for sure who she is, and I am both attracted to, and fearful of the thought of being rejected by, that person right now.

The lore of love's problems is filled with feelings of ambivalence. Courtship ambivalence along the thrill lines of first attraction give way to the dimly thrilling ambivalences of married couples. Intimate relations are likely to give rise to ambivalent feelings (Coser 1964). This ambivalence gives truth to the adage about love and hate being close companions. Both may be present in the agonizing lover. As relationships develop, either love or hate may dominate for a time, but ambivalence is not completely rooted out. It is likely to appear in later stages of intimate lives.

Decisiveness demands more than unambiguous objects. Motivation includes knowledge about intended or likely outcomes from the action. Motivated persons may be sure about the object and what they intend to do, but they

may still feel ambivalent about one of the possible outcomes, intended or unintended, but foreseen nevertheless.
It is also possible to feel ambivalent toward actions because
of what is unknown but feared in free-floating fashion. There
are always unforeseen outcomes. This emotional tug-of-war
is motivational ambivalence: simultaneous attraction to and
repulsion from pursuing a particular line of action.

If motivational ambivalence is strong enough, tension
builds as the person is literally drawn toward and driven
back from a line of action. "Should I or shouldn't I?"
"Whether 'tis better to. . . ." The state of tension is literally
an "agonia," that is, a struggle between opposing actions
within the will and imagination, a personal agony. The
paradigmatic case in the Judeo-Christian traditions may be
Jesus' agony in the garden as he wrestled with his decision
whether to run away or face the anticipated death that
awaited him. "Not my will, but Thine be done."

In the rational milieu of contemporary culture with its
emphasis on clear, distinct, planned, and computerized
ideas, the agony of motivational ambivalence is interpreted
as cognitive breakdown, emotional immaturity, or personal
inadequacy. It must be resolved. For a modern, agony is a
painful condition to be avoided or resolved. Economic rationality would define it paradoxically as a "negative good,"
that is, a counter-productive condition that no rational person would choose.

An individualistic consuming culture teaches that persons are to be happy and life is to be pleasurable. Hedonis-
tic economic rationality defines agony as a morally wrong
"dis-ease" to be avoided as the body avoids disease. Agony
negates the cultural values of optimizing economic or hedo-
nistic rationality. In the modern "battle for human nature,"
individuals are coded genetically, conditioned behaviorally,
and economized rationally, but there is no claim that they
agonize morally (cf. Schwartz 1986).

Agony is distinctly anti-modern. Indeed, moderns are,
perhaps unwittingly, socialized to transform social agony
into personal anxiety. Agony is transmogrified into "my"
anxiety. Social contradictions become personal inadequa-

cies (see Wexler 1983). Anxiety, unlike archaic agony, is a recognized mental health problem befalling individuals. As sick individuals, the anxious can seek rational experts such as counselors, clinicians, and other self-help agents who people the therapeutic sector of modern economies.

Decisiveness requires an ethic of responsibility, that is, a moral weighing of the outcomes of action and recognition of the objective basis for ambivalence. Responsibility evaluates action in terms of the moral status of its outcomes. Given the critical state of the world, an ethics of responsibility must start from an informed recognition of the human condition, of self in the midst of circumstances structured into physical and social processes. When we act, we are responsible to both sets of processes and especially to their interaction. The present focus is on humanly constructed social realities and, for simplicity, on the sources of the circumstances. Feelings, like celestial stars, are physical processes, whereas emotions, like Hollywood stars, are totally social constructions. We are interested in Hollywood objects.

### Ambivalence as a Distinctively Modern Characteristic

Apparently coined in a 1910 article in German, ambivalence was given conceptual force by Sigmund Freud (see Merton and Barber 1963). He used it to interpret the psychodynamics between son and father within the reconstructed family dramas that served as paradigmatic scenes for the birth of psychoanalysis. Freud interpreted the son as both loving and hating his father; as wanting to be close to him and simultaneously rid of him; both seeking his advice and resenting paternal control. In later writings, Freud widened ambivalence to interpret large-scale cultural phenomena as well as interpersonal dynamics, such as client-therapist relations.

The development of the concept within sociological social psychology will be discussed in the next chapter. For now, I want to suggest that the emergence of ambivalence as

an explanatory concept within the psychoanalytic movement and its gradual adoption by sociologists and anthropologists signals a reversal of the relationship between society and personal experience. Instead of socio-cultural
forces channeling contradictory organic and psychic feelings into meaningful patterns, Freud noted that the drama
of socio-cultural forces in the family and beyond can *elicit*
ambivalent feelings. The cultural solution for contradictory
feelings, in other words, has now become the problem.
Underlying our discussion is the proposition: *Modern culture does not effectively resolve ambivalence but increasingly
generates it.*

The psychoanalytic movement, along with other perspectives emerging at the turn of the century, focused on
the reality of subjective life. Emotions were inchoately
taken as objects of their own, rather than as trivial pas-
sions, transcendent forces, or neuro-physiological impulses. Darwin's work on animal expressivity had given evolutionary force to emotional displays and was a precursor of
socio-cultural analysis, not for its explanatory model but for
the importance of organic expressivity. Furthermore, in the
transition from medieval feudalism to contemporary society, social controls no longer offered unquestioned guides
for expressing and understanding experience. Emotional
life became problematic; definitions of feelings became
uncertain; emotions were reconstructed as self-conscious
objects of concern. Cognitive and structural pluralism characteristic of modern life renders futures ambiguous, motivation agonic, decision-making abulic, and emotional relationships ambivalent.

In this modern condition, secondary ambivalence arises. Persons experience *culturally* induced contradictory
feelings toward the same object. Without accepting an overly dualistic ontology of social life, there are arguments for
seeing some cultural facts ordered in binary or contradictory alternatives. The exemplar of secondary multivalence is
here described as ambivalence, that is, the experience of
contradictory emotions toward the same object. We understand multivalence as referring to feelings or affective expe-

riences before they are recognized and socially defined. Ambivalence, on the other hand, refers to contradictory emotions; that is, *contradictory defined feelings*. As contradictory defined feelings, ambivalence is constructed in historically available cultural categories such as love/hate; attraction/repulsion; awe/disdain; joy/sadness; etc. This is ambivalence in the strict sense in which I am using the term.

Ambivalence is an undesirable state for the individual, though it may be functional for a specific structural arrangement. Indeed, an individualistic, competitive, winner-take-all society in which indecision is a character fault is likely to interpret ambivalence as a sign of weak ego, muddled values, or cowardice. Of course, it could signal just the opposite: confidence to confront to both sides of an issue; ability to weigh alternative points of view and give each its probability; and strength to admit that there is no morally certain line of action. Ambivalence is not the problem. Rather, it is the indecision that may follow and block action. The problem is abulia, although the pain is ambivalence.

Robert Merton's sociological analyses (1976; 1983) suggest that ambivalence can result from contradictory normative expectations within a role, role set, or status, and that it can be functional for the social system within which it occurs. For example, a successful doctor should be both warm interpersonally and cool diagnostically, both supportive of the patient's needs and demanding of compliance to the medical regimen. Likewise, a creatively productive scientist must act in accord with universalistic rules of measurement, data, evidence, and logic. At the same time, a good scientist must remain open to the unexpected, or even stubbornly adhere to hunch or bias in pursuit of better instrumentation, design, or interpretation. Analogously, the competent parent both nurtures the child's explorations and holds firm to limits on the child's conduct; both protects the child and exposes it to increasing risk.

An important question is whether the functionality of ambivalence for the social system it is also functional for the individual. The original psychoanalytic use of ambivalence seems to assume that it is a stressful condition from which the sufferer seeks escape, e.g., in religious or ideological certainty. As we shall see below, phenomenologists of religion find ambivalence at the heart of sacred experience and suggest that institutional religion offers socially constructed solutions to this perennial issue. In interaction with persons who are not like us, there is some evidence that ambivalent attitudes lead to over-reactions. It is as though persons seek to resolve ambivalence by overly embracing one of their emotional tendencies. These leads suggest that the ambivalent condition is stressful and motivates a search for resolution through a variety of responses: punitive (Katz 1981), joking (Coser 1966), counter-cultural (Yinger 1982), religious (Otto 1958), or "normally neurotic" (Putney and Putney 1972). Whether these responses are beneficial for society or the individual is an empirical question. Let us review some instances.

Analyses of professions show functional ambivalence. Since contradictory normative expectations bind the doctor and scientist, an ambivalent professional performs more effectively than someone who acts according to one norm and disregards the contradictory one, e.g., the competent but coldly rejecting doctor; the technically skilled but unimaginative scientist. The successful professional creatively works through the ambivalence generated by the structured tension of contradictory norms. Similar tension radiates through the properly controlling versus supporting parent interacting with increasingly independent but not yet competent children.

In a dramaturgical analysis of airline flight attendants, mainly women, Arlie Hochschild (1983) sketches an ambivalence that is disfunctional for the individual and hardly beneficial for the occupation, even though it may be functional for the airline's control of its employees. She coins the construct "emotional labor" to grasp the "product" that the female flight attendant fashions for the client. The attendant must keep smiling, no matter what happens.

The smile symbolizes the airline's acceptance of the passenger, no matter how obnoxious the passenger is

toward the attendant. The emotional labor needed to produce this smile for mile after mile regardless of the attendant's real feelings demands deep acting. Such acting allows
the attendant to display a feeling that contradicts her angry
experience. The attendant learns to separate her feelings
from her presentation of emotion face to face with dirty or
drunk passengers. The job demands that she produce a
smile and feign a self which she does not feel. "'Your smile is
your biggest asset—use it.' In demonstrating how to deal
with . . . passengers who are sick or flirtatious or otherwise
troublesome, a trainer held up a card that said, 'Relax and
smile'" (Hochschild 1983: 105). Deep ambivalence is controlled to sustain the institutional definition: the customer
is always right, and I want him to fly me. This control exacts
a disfunctionally high price from the attendant who eventually suffers burnout or gradually retreats from the presenta-
tional demands of the job as she searches for her authentic
feeling self.

In wide-ranging anthropological analyses of traditional
African peoples whose lives are disrupted, Peter Marris
(1975) interprets ambivalence as a functional buffer for all
who face deep change. He sees ambivalence based on
"instinctual" conservative responses to tragic personal loss
or scary social change. People find themselves with new
tasks thrust upon them, or they see cherished goods torn
from them. In such transitions, people both cling to feelings
for the cherished objects now lost and try to accept the new
reality of their situation. Experiential continuity and situational reality come together in ambivalent feelings that
"reach before and after," as they live with what is and yearn
for what is no longer. His analyses highlight the ambivalence-generating nature of the "social life process" that
underlies our existence (cf. Mead 1934).

Persons faced with the destruction of their village,
forced relocation, death, or divorce experience ambivalence between the old and the present, between traditional
values and the exigencies of today. Ambivalence toward
changed situations appears as an inevitable, indeed, normal
confrontation between the consolation of the known past

and the threat of the imagined future. Such ambivalence characterizes the psychological stage between the old and the new, and the struggle to give meaning to bewildering events. Some may resolve the struggle by embracing the new with open arms and rejecting the past, others by violently resisting the new and clinging to the past. Unresolved ambivalence can lead to over-reaction by the person or group. If ambivalence remains unresolved for too long and the distress finds collective expression, it may motivate excessively violent responses.

The possibility of violence is consistent with the perspective of those who interpret ambivalence as a form of social pathology causing deeply felt discontent (Thom 1984). Although at first glance such an interpretation appears plausible and may fit some situations, it is not the theoretical avenue followed here. The social pathology interpretation implies that ambivalence results from individual or societal defect. It locates ambivalence in the same domain as social illnesses such as anomie, alienation, or exploitation. The present argument, on the other hand, posits primary ambivalence as an anthropological possibility rooted in a philosophical understanding of the relatively instinctless nature of the human organism. As such, it is hardly the result of faulty social organization or unauthentic culture that could be set right by social engineering. Indeed, one philosopher argues that ambivalence may be a reasonable mode of human action (Greenspan 1980).

Secondary or sociological ambivalence results in part from the pluralism, value relativity, and increasing technological control in everyday life. Ambivalence is deepened by widening military, technological, and industrial consequences that place species survival in the balance. Whether a particular ambivalence and its objects are basically pathological, or in a more limited sense, functional or disfunctional for the individual or society remains an empirical question, not a theoretical given. A particular ambivalence may point to a pathological situation; e.g., feeling drawn to and repulsed by the existence of more nuclear bombs than are needed to destroy life on earth, yet others see the same

objects as positive tactical chips in geopolitical games, or
neutral technical puzzles needing solution.

We do not interpret ambivalence as a sure sign of
social pathology. Rather, sociological ambivalence is generated by processes that analysts consider neutral, perhaps
good, and maybe inevitable. These processes include: a
bewildering array of choices; communication that is becoming laser quick; knowledge production increasing geometri-
cally; more frequent and quicker travel; and the increased
scope of technology into every ecological niche with ever
longer reach into the future of natural systems. Think of
supermarkets, computers, rockets, satellites, and above all,
environmental intervention and nuclear bombs. Different
results may be judged desirable or undesirable, but the
mixed outcomes do not definitely and irrevocably brand the
processes as evil. An ethic of responsibility wrestles with
mixed results as its normal moral task. To expect anything
else is to short change life. There are no pat emotions in the
face of mixed results. Ambivalence, then, may be a well-
informed and intellectually courageous response to the pluralistic complexity of contemporary life.

## Ambivalence and Self-Consciousness

Whatever its moral worth, ambivalence generates a
particularly modern sense of self-consciousness. In a preliminary phenomenology of ambivalence, Kenneth Shapiro
(1985: 171–209) finds the experience within ordinary living
and describes different levels of response, e.g., intellectual-
izing the experience and translating it into a rational decision matrix; or submersion in a vortex of personal conflict
so that no action is possible. He ends by locating ambivalence within a living dialectic. One way of moving through
life creatively is by relating to both poles of ambivalence
without explaining either away. "A genuine resolution of
ambivalence displaces it with a dialectic..., a bodily way of
living, abstracting, and understanding" (209). Beyond
resolved ambivalent experience lies another and another.

To live fully, then, we must respond to ambivalent situations by absorbing them creatively.

Experiencing ambivalence heightens awareness toward self, the environment, and possible courses of action. The tension of ambivalence is part of the motivational price of wrestling with reality, whether it comes in the form of an angel or a devil. Paraphrasing that exemplar of American consciousness, Captain Ahab, who intoned that his means are sane, it is his goal that is mad, we could suggest that we are sane, it is society that is mad. The structural madness places individuals in that no-win Catch 22 situation that symbolizes the modern predicament. A radical critique would argue that society defines normality, yet an individual who fits the criteria of normal is thereby rendered mad according to meta-societal criteria.

In a word, a society built on contradictory imperatives elicits ambivalence. An extension of this leitmotif is that ambivalence puts the individual in touch with transcendence, or at least with an experience that can be textualized and interpreted as uncanny, eerie, fascinating, and generative of heightened awareness. A plausible line of speculation is as follows. From a social constructionist perspective, it is not the "real," objective, or personal presence of a numinous entity that grounds the experience of the sacred that then elicits ambivalence. Rather, it is the contradictory affective situation that elicits ambivalence that is then resolved by a symbolic being which reconciles the opposites. Phenomenologists speak of the natural attitude that constitutes experience of the mundane world. This world is characterized by unquestioned attributions of reality to causes, real beings, and living persons, which attributions allow persons to experience themselves as being for real, leading normal lives, and able to navigate their daily rounds with minimal threat and anxiety. Disruptions to this mundaneity can be interpreted as intrusions of transcendence, whether divine or diabolical, natural or unnatural, moral or perverse. The leap is to argue or at least posit, ex hypothesi, that such intrusions are generated by the ambivalent imperatives of institutions, interaction, or nature's forces.

Once experienced, ambivalence affectively keys a problematic situation (Hewitt and Hall 1973). Mundaneity is interrupted; a problematic situation emerges. The actor does not know what to think, how to feel, or which course of action to pursue. The self is abulic; the body stops in a stutter step. Problematic situations generate self-consciousness that leads to a search for cognitive solutions. In contradictory situations, self is likely also to have mixed feelings. Actors struggling to return to mundaneity search not only for clarity but also for comfort. The emergent self-consciousness seeks a practical form of certainty, enough to get on with life, but in a context characterized by heightened "attention to life" (see Schutz 1962). The normal person in an ambivalent problematic situation, then, is analogous to the marginal person. The ambivalent person is "marginalized" from the culture of mundaneity, that is, he or she is no longer cosseted in normality. Rather, the ambivalent is uncertain, anxious, divided, and momentarily unsure how self is relevant to the situation. From a strictly social psychological viewpoint, the self does not know Who I am. Ambivalence disturbs the practical salience hierarchy of identities that routinely deals with the demands of the situation. The hierarchy of identities needs to be reshuffled.

Normality defines a mode of consciousness that allows the human animal to go about its daily routines with predictable energy expenditure. The lifeworld is felt as mundane reality: routine, unquestioned, with focused and reasonably efficient use of life force. This entire configuration of the existential attitude to the world is what we mean by the phrase, attention to life. Mundane attention to life virtually submerges attention into the institutionalized routines and personal habits that carry the self ever closer to the end of organic life. As pragmatic thinkers have put the issue from the other side, consciousness arises as the organism is confronted with a problematic situation in which goals, means, perceptions, and feelings are suddenly unreachable, ineffective, ambiguous, or ambivalent. In everyday life, our routines are interrupted as we stumble into a "problematic situation" that sociologists unpack as a problem of knowledge and action: How do I know what am I to do? We need also to ask: What am I to feel? The effective commingling of experience presents self with a problem: Who am I if I do not know What I am feeling? Commingled feelings are part of confused thinking and both obstruct concerted action. In stark form, such mixed emotions or ambivalence generate ambiguity and anxiety toward self, other, and action, and ambiguity cum anxiety heightens, not just consciousness, but self-consciousness. Ambivalence, as a form of affective life, adds deep emotional experience to that characteristic of modern pluralism: heightened self-consciousness and moral anxiety about Who am I and What am I to do.

Arguing from analogy, ambivalence as a form of modern life renders us marginal in a way evocative of those fascinating social types, the stranger, the outsider, the marginal person. Just as one inherited interpretation of the Protestant Reformation states that Martin Luther was able to destroy institutionalized monasteries and convents by taking the stone cloister walls and transforming them into psychological walls of guilt within conscience, so the shift to modernity takes the class and ethnic differences underwriting social distinctions and transforms them into emotional and ideological differences co-existing within consciousness.

From Goffman's dramaturgical perspective, everyone with a personal attribute that others evaluate negatively in the situation is stigmatized (1963: 106–8). And every stigmatized person is thereby ambivalent to the stigmatized part of self. A speculative extension of Goffman's argument states that the atomistic individualism of American society renders each person morally and empirically responsible for personal fate, even for one's evaluation in the eyes of others. Yet, no individual is perfect. If self were to think so, time forces every form of perfection to pass later if not sooner. In an individualistic culture, every person is or will feel stigmatized publically or privately. Once stigmatized, persons are seen to be in ambivalent situations, or must manage the secret information that they think they are in ambivalent situations, even if others do not know it. Stigmatized moderns must learn to interact in such a way that desired definitions of the situation and courses of action are successfully sustained. Those with apparent stigmas of body, gesture, talk, or clothes learn how to "normalize" interaction with non-apparently stigmatized others so that the scene can come off without destroying either self, other, or the joint activity. Persons with non-apparent stigmas that need to be kept hidden are faced with deeper dramaturgical problems of controlling information about the stigma and managing one's performance to create the positive but inaccurate impression of being a non-stigmatized self.

A downwardly mobile unemployed ex-manager, for example, constructs a resumé that creates the impression of continuous high-level employment couched in the proper executive jargon (Newman 1989: 81–2). The unemployed learn that papered appearances become fate. Similarly, employed working class persons caught on the objective contradictions of personal achievement versus group solidarity and the internal contradictions of badges of self worth that are arbitrarily ignored by authoritarian superiors feel ambivalence at the heart of self (Sennett and Cobb 1973). Even categorical identities generate ambivalence if they manifest minority status in a nation state that both claims universal civic equality and enforces particularistic paths to power, wealth, and status (Dench 1986). At the extreme, such state logic for both delegitimating and discriminating against minorities leads to their definition as deviants. The "deviantizing" tactic is a degradation move that stigmatizes minorities as justly liable objects of state coercion and violence (cf. Schur 1980). The availability of social and culture stigmas and the power of the modern state to employ its reality-producing rhetoric to deviantize minorities and any category of members, as the recent administration did to air controllers and many administrations do to reform movements such as peace protesters, create stigma in its citizens. Stigma, however, renders self ambivalent to one's own self. Here is a powerful way in which a class-based nation state founded on meritocratic individualism can generate ambivalence in each of us.

## *Summary*

Thinking about ambivalence as a characteristic of modern feeling uncovers the complexity of its causes, consequences, and functionality. That is why I am taking a chance with this book. It is a rather undefended essay, not a final proof. Hopefully, if read benignly, it will stimulate others to deepen understanding of the temper of our times. No positivistic exercise in abstracted empiricism, or interpretive foray into escapist theorizing will do. We need to consider the costs of feeling ambivalent, as well as the costs of breaking away from mixed feelings.

The discussion builds on the simple axiom that self-understanding and self-organization are functions of society and social organization. This axiom is usually applied to the way we think and act; it is also applicable to the way we feel. The structure and experience of emotions reflect the structure and effects of social organization—this is one of the messages of the sociology of emotions. I wish to strengthen this development by interpreting contemporary ambivalence as a case in point.

Ambivalence is not totally functional for the individual qua individual. It is typically a distressful condition. The distress may lead to extreme responses as the ambivalent sufferer tries to resolve the emotional dilemma by embracing one of the contradictory objects. As motivation to extreme responses, ambivalence is potentially dangerous, especially in an age of enhanced instruments of violence, whether to self or other. Ambivalence may characterize personal or group dynamics, and it may lead to individual or collective responses. Willy-nilly, moderns must cope with mixed emotions.

Ambivalence can be functional for larger social arrangements at least for the time being. To understand ambivalence, individuals need to personalize social controls and to socialize personal feelings. Ambivalence generated by contradictory expectations in modern institutions is a consequence of the complexity of society and creates mobile and malleable moderns.

If the pace of social change is increasing, so too must the cognitive and emotional ability to change our selves (Zurcher 1977). But do we so change that we cease entirely to be what we were, either as individuals or as a community? Robert Bellah and associates (1985) argue that moral ambivalence is a sign that the dominant utilitarian individualism of American society has not yet absorbed traditional sources of moral sentiments. May it be that lingering ambivalence among modern Americans is functional for moral and cultural renewal? Such speculation calls for attention. Berger (1980), for example, sees modern life calling believers to be "heretics," i.e., to make fateful cognitive choices. May it not be that moderns are called to be "affective heretics" as well, to follow one emotion while feeling others of equal strength?

Whether we praise or blame the experience of mixed emotions, ambivalence is characteristic of the life and arrangements of modern society. We need to understand its causes and consequences, recognize its potential danger for generating extreme responses, and turn its distressful power into creative motivation. We must begin to think of the person as *animal ambivalens* and accept our Janus-faced condition. This book is but a halting first step. The next chapter contains traces of a more systematic sociological path toward understanding mixed emotions.

# Chapter 2

◻

# Ambivalence as a Social Reality*

Contrary to what we take as medieval wisdom, it is not likely that Buridan's ass, placed equally distant between identically appealing piles of hay, would experience equal forces pulling in each direction and starve to death. This sad outcome is unlikely for several reasons: an animal would have an instinctual or sensory mechanism for responding to that situation; and more to the point, equality and identity are idealized symbolic transformations found only in the realm of abstraction and not in the physical world. As geometers are fond of reminding us, there are no such physical realities like a point, line, circle, or square as defined in their world. Not an ass, but a relatively instinct-less being that lives in a symbolically transformed world may starve to death if placed equally distant between two identical goals, or at least suffer intense anxiety, uncertainty, and indecisiveness. It is the human who is an "ambivalent animal" (Shapiro 1968).

In so far as ambivalence accompanies uncertainty and indecisiveness, it further weakens that structure of understandings and emotional attachments through which we define our situation and sustain a sense of who we are. Clearly interpreted emotion is an important cue for the for-

*From the original co-authored chapter "Ambivalence: A Touchstone of the Modern Temper," in THE SOCIOLOGY OF EMOTIONS: ORIGINAL ESSAYS AND RESEARCH PAPERS, edited by David D. Franks and E. Doyle McCarthy, JAI Press, 1989, pp. 205-227.

mation of a coherent personal identity (Hochschild 1983: 32). Without firm feelings toward who we are, action is hesitant, halting, and truncated. Predictable, validating responses from others are blocked. Yet, such responses are the bedrock of that source of self-esteem that comes from a sense of competence and efficacious action (see Cooley 1964; Franks and Marolla 1976; Gecas and Schwalbe 1983; White 1965).

Ambivalence is not conceived here as a unitary and primary emotion. The experience is constituted by two or more incompatible emotions. This incompatibility is generated on at least two levels. The first is cognitive and results from the symbol-based recognition of logical contradiction. Hochschild (1979) speaks of "secondary acts performed on the nonreflective stream of primary emotive experience." As mentioned above, emotions are feelings defined as meaningful. If the conceptual labels used to interpret primary emotive experiences contradict each other, the result is blunted emotions. Neither dominates experience.

The second level of incompatibility is action. Emotion involves bodily, sentient preparation for particular action (Hochschild 1983: 220). Antithetical emotions would require antithetical actions that would block each other. A person cannot approach and flee simultaneously without breaking apart. Since acting out emotions strengthens them for a time, fully felt affect is weakened for the ambivalent person. Emotional life would go on anxious hold. The ambivalent person experiences the deep gray of contradictory feelings; of inconsistent knowledge; and of the indeterminateness of mutually exclusive decisions to act. Ambivalence refers to an emotional state when: I can't decide what to do; I don't know what to think about my experience; I have mixed feelings about this action.

Ambivalence is an outrider of intense social change for symbol-using animals such as we are. Furthermore, ideas and tools do not emerge haphazardly: the coinage and adoption of ambivalence at the dawn of the twenty-first century imply institutional arrangements and personal needs that offer insight into today's world (see Coser and Rosenberg 1976). If ambivalence is a particularly modern issue, then many voices need to address it from sociobiology through psychoanalysis and on to history. Our focus is on sociological and social psychological angles. Whether ambivalence is functional for institutional arrangements is left open, but it appears that ambivalence is personally distressful.

We start our sociological story by noting adumbrations in some early sociological authors at about the same time Freud used the idea of ambivalence. Then we sketch its development at different levels of more contemporary sociological analysis. The discussion leads to a schematic generalized model of social antecedents of ambivalence. A preliminary bridge between social structure and personal experience comes from Hochschild's social psychological work (especially 1983). Finally, we trace the range of ambivalence and emphasize its usefulness for understanding what it means to be modern. Following chapters provide applications to more specific issues.

### Generic Sources of Ambivalence:
### Change, Incompleteness, and Complexity

There may be universal feeling responses built into the protoplasmic substratum of the human animal. Even if such biological programming is built in, however, it does not provide fixed objects for feelings. Biological programming cannot explain socially selected feelings of the beloved for the lover, or of the Democrat for the Republican. Only some children recoil in disgust from slimy icky things that live under rocks. Even if we assume that disgust and its class of objects are biologically programmed, there is no conceivable biological predetermination that makes Republicans or newts feel disgust in the presence of non-slimy but liberal Democrats. The meaning of such objects is socially constructed and learned; renegotiation and change are possible.

Change is the soil for ambivalence. Change simultaneously creates both the excitement of novelty and fright for familiar routines. The person can yearn for what the future may bring and yet mourn for the past that future will destroy. Our tragically short bodily presence demands that the transformation of the baby into a person is a never-ending passage through social institutions and personal identities. Changes that work through social roles and personal socialization are clearly socially created; however, the linearity of organic life is a kind of time that imposes physical change on us whether we wish it or not, and whether or not it is institutionalized, like aging, illness, or accident. Aging is change come home to roost. The reality of change and the linear temporality of organic life generates experiential ambivalence in the lives of even the most prim and proper persons.

Understanding life as temporal process means that knowledge of and action toward others as well as self is never complete. We strive to interact meaningfully with others about whom we know next to nothing or think we know all—until a depressing or delightful discovery changes our relationship. We routinely "fill in" our incomplete knowledge of others with social stuff by seeing them as typical actors with whom we can safely interact in typical ways.

Even as we fill in others, we are potentially aware that we do not know them, or ourselves, completely. In critical junctures, awareness of incomplete knowledge divides our relationship: do I relate to the other as known or as unknown? Such structured ignorance generates a dialectic of trust-distrust in each other (Barber 1983; Lewis and Weigert 1985). Persons are defined by what they are or have been, but also by what they are not yet. To be human is paradoxically to be defined by the about-to-be-future (Ortega 1964). It sounds odd, but we are defined by what we are not yet. Is this not the heart of promises, contracts, friendship, marriage, parenthood? Since perception is selective and limited by our biographical standpoint, knowledge is necessarily incomplete. Ambivalence stands just around the corner from incomplete knowledge.

Social relations are a complex fusion of interpretations by self, others, and impersonal forces (Blasi et al. 1978). This multi-hued fusion of social realities is linked to ambivalence (cf. Hajda 1968; Schutz 1964: 227). Emotions like love or hate are precarious transformations of changing, incomplete, and complex experience. Consider a woman constructing her love for a man. Does she love him as he is now but will eventually no longer be, or as he will become but is not yet (cf. Ortega 1976)? If she chooses to love him as he is now, will she come to hate who he is in the process of becoming by ceasing to be who he is now—precisely the objectified person she now loves. Or is it possible for her—or for you or me—to stand emotionally naked before the object of her love as another changing, incomplete, complex person, and to feel as a single experience the confluence of contradictory feelings, and to transform that ambivalence into committed love outlasting any future?

As society changes more rapidly; as increased population densities render mutual knowledge increasingly incomplete; and as social relations and institutions are more open to competing and complex definitions, we expect that ambivalence would increase (cf. Merton 1976). Some evidence from political surveys suggests that ambivalent attitudes exist among the general population. Yankelovich (1982) writes, "Though they exhibit different moods, one expansive, the other apprehensive, the two current public states of mind do coexist: Americans are hopeful and fearful at the same time" (185). These coexisting contradictory moods create "an almost intolerable level of tension and confusion." Yankelovich quotes Amitai Etzioni to the effect that "in the long run, such high ambivalence is too stressful for societies to endure" (185–6). A Marxist perspective on contemporary crisis in "late" capitalist societies finds that economic, social, and political ambiguities typically generate "ambivalent mass attitudes" that tend to undermine the process of accumulation so important to the capitalist system (O'Connor 1987: 151–2). Such hints strengthen interpretations of American institutions as structured with contradictory values (cf. Turner and Musick 1985). It is helpful to consider contradictory imperatives from the perspectives of sociology, a discipline that emerged with the conflict accompanying the transition to modernity.

*Some Early Roots: Ambivalence and the Twentieth Century*

Acknowledging that Bleuler coined the term about 1910, Freud used ambivalence to refer to the experience of simultaneous contradictory emotions (see 1915/1964: 131 fn). He sees it as characteristic of relations of intimacy, of narcissistic tendencies, and of taboos (1923/1961: 42; 1916–7/1964: 427–8; 1913/1964: 32). On the one hand, thinking of a kind of instinctual reality, he "suggests the probability that the *psychical impulses of primitive peoples were characterized by a higher amount of ambivalence than is found in modern civilized man*" (1913/1964: 66, his italics). On the other hand, in later reflections on socio-cultural processes in *Civilization and its Discontents,* he states:

> if civilization is a necessary course of development from the family to humanity as a whole, then—as a result of the inborn conflict arising from ambivalence, of the eternal struggle between the trends of love and death—there is inextricably bound up with it an increase of the sense of guilt, which will perhaps reach heights that the individual finds hard to tolerate (1930/1964: 133).

In other words, even if moderns are freer of ambivalent "psychical impulses," they are driven by an ever stronger emotion of guilt arising from social ambivalence generated by the increasing complexity and responsibility of "civilized" persons. Freud presciently, for a pre-nuclear reflection, ends that book with a profound worry whether the trends of love can triumph over hate now that the latter is served by weapons sufficient to kill every woman, man, and child.

Classical sociological writers during Freud's lifetime do not appear to use ambivalence as a self-conscious theoretical term. Central themes in early sociology, however, were the contradictory effects of the transition to modernity on individual consciousness and of the conflict between tradition and rationality. The dialectical, ironical, and conflict analyses of Marx, Weber, and Simmel suggest the potential fruitfulness of ambivalence for sociological analyses. Emile

Durkheim, for example, concludes a discussion of the homo duplex thesis as follows:

> Therefore, since the role of the social being in our single selves will grow ever more important as history moves ahead, it is wholly improbable that there will ever be an era in which man is required to resist himself to a lesser degree, an era in which he can live life that is easier and less full of tension. To the contrary, all evidence compels us to expect our effort in the struggle between the two beings within us to increase with the growth of civilization (1964: 339).

Durkheim's sense of an increasing struggle within the social self corroborates Freud's psychological argument.

From an institutional point of view, Norbert Elias analyzes what he calls "the civilizing process" and offers the thesis that the transition from feudal society to modern centralized states was facilitated by an "ambivalence of interests" that developed within medieval society. He argues that increasing social complexity introduced a "special quality" into social relationships characterized by competing obligations. That quality is a sense of ambivalence accompanying the interweaving of interests as individuals became more interdependent and each stratum became functionally involved within more differentiated social systems. He states:

> this fundamental ambivalence of interests, its consequences in political life or psychological make-up, and its sociogenesis in relation to advancing division of functions ... (is) one of the most important structural characteristics of more highly developed societies, and a chief factor moulding civilized conduct (1982: 168, his italics).

This judgment, that moderns exist at the intersection of competing demands, was originally published in 1939. It picks up earlier social themes such as a Simmelian social self and it foreshadows later analyses, particularly Robert Merton's discussion of the paragons of "civilized" types, namely, professionals.

### *A Sociological Argument: Ambivalence as Social Reality*

Psychoanalytic thinking, parent-child identification and therapist-patient transference involve simultaneous emotions of love and hate as the dependent person struggles for autonomy. Sociologists began to notice ambivalence within less intense relationships such as those between teachers and supervisors in educational bureaucracies (Seeman 1953). This analysis suggests that ambivalence is a general feature of dominance or leadership positions as incumbents strive to be both respected and liked, authoritative and nurturant, or evaluative and supportive toward the same person. In his reformulations of Simmel's work on social conflict, Lewis Coser (1956) theorizes that ambivalence is a potential feature of all intimate relations, not just those between parent and child. Erving Goffman goes further and posits ambivalence as a general dramaturgical feature in presenting ourselves to others. He states:

> Shared staging problems; concern for the way things appear; warranted and unwarranted feelings of shame; ambivalence about oneself and one's audience: these are some of the dramaturgic elements of the human situation (1959: 237).

Sociological ambivalence is caused by contradictory demands built into social organizations as well as face to face encounters. In a well-known article on social structure and anomie, Robert Merton noted that ambivalence caused by conflict between the demands of the situation and internalized norms that are no longer relevant can fan pangs of conscience in those who violate them (1949: 379). He also saw ambivalence as a fundamental feature of bureaucracy (154). Developing the idea of reference groups as essential supports for a sense of identity, he suggested that ambivalence between old and new group ties may explain why new recruits often become super members more committed to the group than born members. Further, Merton noted that ambivalence leads to amplified commitment so that converts adamantly adhere to the new faith more strongly than born believers (1957: 295). In this context, he quotes Talcott Parsons: "alienation is conceived *always* to be part of an ambivalent motivational structure, while conformity need not be" (*The Social System:* 254, his italics). We hypothesize that over-conformity may result from an attempt to resolve alienating ambivalence by overly embracing one of the emotional alternatives.

In a 1963 article, Merton and Barber further codified ambivalence as a technical term. They distinguished sociological ambivalence from its psychological and psychoanalytic uses. Mertonian analysis recognizes the links among social organization, individual motivation, and social action. Ties between social structure and the self ground his most fertile observations. For example, in large-scale organizations, the contradictory demands of regularity and creativity can result in a kind of bureaucratic pathos. The unrequitable demands for empathic personal concern versus rational universalistic detachment pose acute problems and generate deep tensions. Merton frequently looked at the contradictory demands placed on the exemplary cultural carriers of the modern world, namely, science and medicine, and generalized them to the top occupational stratum, the professions themselves.

In a pluralistic society, persons are positioned within multiple status sets and reference groups that exert pressures for contradictory actions. The physician is not only an autonomous professional, but increasingly, also a conforming member of an occupational bureaucracy such as a medical team or hospital. She may also be a mother and wife, not to mention card-carrying Democrat. Earlier, she was a dependent obedient student before becoming a relatively autonomous doctor. Previous status characteristics are likely to have residual effects. It takes time for motives and feelings to change from student and female dependency to professional autonomy.

Each status that the physician possesses and each identity through which she knows herself have sets of roles that may make contradictory demands on feelings, motives,

and action. The physician is expected to be concerned for
each patient as a person, and yet detached enough to make
difficult decisions, like the triage-type decisions that in
effect determine how long this or that person may go on living. She must have "detached concern." The same individual who happens to be a physician is simultaneously a healer,
scientist, businessperson, and caring person. Finally, each
role in itself may combine contradictory expectations that
can be met in only a partial way by a single course of action.
As healer, the doctor may impose hard regimens or easy
ones; as a scientist, she may pursue pharmacological, surgi-
cal, or holistic hypotheses; as a businessperson, she may
charge whatever the market will bear or hold down costs to
serve the less rich; and as a caring person, she may grieve
for the fate of the dying or destitute. A physician alert to the
alternatives may indeed experience ambivalence.

Merton and Barber define core sociological ambivalence as *"conflicting normative expectations socially defined
for a particular social role associated with a single social status"* (1963; 1976: 8, their italics). Faced with conflicting
expectations, the person in the status, whether doctor,
bureaucrat, parent, student, or whoever, cannot conform to
a norm and a counter norm in the same behavior. Yet,
ambivalence must be resolved for action to occur. The role
incumbent can block out one norm and embrace the other,
perhaps overzealously to keep the rejected norm from inter-
jecting itself; or the person can oscillate between actions
that meet now one norm, now the other. Exaggerated or
oscillating actions portray sociological ambivalence.

Although both contradictory ideas and contradictory
feelings may be experienced together, it is important to dis-
tinquish between knowing ambiguity and feeling ambivalence. Contradictory norms are likely to elicit both responses. There are times in which the course of action is clear but
the emotional response to it is ambivalent, as when a parent
knows that the child must be allowed greater autonomy in
spite of fear for the danger: the adolescent's first solo in the
family car. There are cases in which the emotion is clear but
the course of action is not. Parents may feel unambivalent

love for their child, but they still do not know whether to discipline or nurture her here and now. It appears that ambiguity and ambivalence can cause each other. Both, furthermore, are derived from socio-cultural characteristics of complex situations.

We use the term, psychological ambivalence, to refer explicitly to the contradictory experience or characteristics of individuals, rather than to socio-cultural contradictions. Psychological ambivalence stands between socio-cultural contradictions and the decisions and actions of individuals. Instances of psychological ambivalence have been analyzed as conflicting emotions, contradictory attitudes, conflicting definitions of self or other, and contradictory relationships between intimates or within groups (e.g., Bardwick and Douvan 1971; Coser 1964; Coser, 1966; Goffman 1963; Katz 1981; Katz et al. 1977; Slater and Slater 1965; Wiseman 1976). Psychological ambivalence is a construct at the individual level of analysis. It can be transformed into instances of humor, though standard research practice may mask its presence (Anderson and Wieting 1976). Once identified, psychological ambivalence can be conceptualized both as an independent variable or "cause" influencing decisions and actions, and as a dependent variable or "effect" resulting from socio-cultural forces.

Within a rational, instrumental, and success-oriented culture, psychological ambivalence is distressfully anomalous. In an ethos of success, tough mindedness and surety of purpose are cultural imperatives. Successful people are not slowed by doubt or mixed feelings. Ambivalence is not allowed to surface in the first place, or if felt, it must be overridden quickly. Failure to do so can be interpreted as a lack of strong ego, firm identity, or even as a touch of abnormality: a sort of stressed "wimpiness."

A society with utilitarian individualism and personal autonomy as core values sees unresolved ambivalence as pathological weakness at the heart of self (cf. Bellah 1976). We argue that interpreting ambivalence as individual failure makes adequate self-understanding impossible. Erik Erikson argues that identity integration and continuity throughout life is a definitive task for the contemporary self to understand and, even more, strive to achieve (1959; 1978; and Lifton 1980). To be sure, if self has no predictable or understandable emotional structure, then effective interaction and meaningful interpretation of one's life is impossible. The social meaning of an individual's life embodies an emotional involvement in an imagined future as a necessary component of responsible decisions and actions (Blumer 1969; Schutz 1967). To the extent that psychological ambivalence interferes with imagining efficacious futures to which we are emotionally drawn, it weakens motivation, blocks decisions, inhibits action, generates anxiety, and results in existential dis-ease that eventually sparks a search for a solution.

From a sociological perspective, psychological ambivalence results, not from personal sickness, but from cultural, institutional, interactional, or social psychological factors. As we explore sociological sources, we will invariably imply these psychological states of individuals and the experiential consequences of sociological ambivalence. Discussion of contradictions in values, norms, or identities must touch on individual experience as well. The interpretive focus, however, displays these experiential phenomena as reflections of socio-cultural realities.

## Levels of Sociological Ambivalence

What follows is not an exhaustive review of studies of ambivalence. Rather, it illustrates the kinds of studies found at different levels of socio-cultural analysis.

### A. Culture

Milton Yinger (1982) suggests that ambivalence is built into cultural life as a result of contradictory central values that generate the historical dialectic of culture-counterculture. A visible component of complex societies is groups whose beliefs and ways of life announce values and identities that contradict those of the official culture. Yinger

states that ambivalence is a key concept for unlocking countercultural dynamics as diverse as movements for black
identity, patterns of delinquency, and experiments in communal living (127). His interpretive descriptions are consistent with the hint from Berger et al. (1973: 110) that modernity both demands partial or "componential" selves in
response to the complex specialization of society, and re-
enforces traditional claims for a sense of authentic personal
wholeness—contradictory cultural imperatives that intensi-
fy personal ambivalence.

Indeed, the ideology of achieved individual success as
a primary right and of inherent individual privilege as a concomitant but contradictory right locates ambivalence at the
heart of society (cf. Ichheiser 1970). Surveying the American scene shows long-standing tensions between, for example, immigrants' attachment to the old country and love for
the new, and contemporaries' demands for both total autonomy and increasing entitlement to certain standards of
health and well-being (see Morawska 1987; Yankelovich
1982).

## B. Organization

Analysts of bureaucracy and the professions find
further evidence of ambivalence. Combining a functional
and interpretive perspective, Cohn (1960) tries to make
sense out of the simultaneous contradictory judgments
patients make about doctors whom they both deeply
admire and severely criticize. Cohn argues that high status
occupations combine two opposed and yet related sets of
values, namely, privileges of high status and the gifts of
charisma. In response to the combined values, the patient
interprets the medical professional as both a profit-seeking
business person and as a wonderful enlightened healer.
Contradictory qualities attributed to the same identity elicit
both awe and respect from those in a position of dependency who seek healing. Patients both feel that they are in the
presence of some kind of supra-mundane power, and are
willing, nay, eager at times, to pay heavily for its application
to their well-being. Patients' "mundane awe" complements

the "detached concern" characteristic of the doctor. The healing relationship forks ambivalently at each end.

Increasing bureaucratization and specialization within the medical professions may lessen ambivalence from the status-charisma tension while increasing it from other tensions. A dialect of trust-distrust, for example, may so deepen ambivalence that it moves patients to seek redress through the courts and litigation (Lewis and Weigert 1985; Lieberman 1981). Bureaucratized professionals feel the tension between predictable conformity to bureaucratic rules, and the creative autonomy of professional competence.

Within the scientific community, there is the unending tug of war between imperatives to follow impersonal universalistic norms of methodology, theory, and evidence, and on the other hand, to follow personal particularistic norms of emotional involvement, hunch, or even bias (Merton 1976; Mitroff 1974). In spite of models of how science is supposed to work ideally, the practices of successful scientists show that the tension between norm-counternorm provides a necessary dynamic. This suggests analogies with the adversarial procedures of arriving at truth in the forensic practices of courts of law, or the philosophical dialectic of argumentation and controversy. As has been said, one well-worked error may contribute more to generating knowledge than a multitude of luke-warm truths.

## C. Family

Within the small world of family, the tension a person feels between individual and group needs takes on special intensity. Group members seek both the autonomy and profit that our individualistic culture holds so dear, and the security and commonweal that everyone needs and the group provides. There are payoffs and costs in the pursuit of either goal, and the calculations are intricately complex for the person who tries to achieve both. Cultural values teach the individual to work hard for personal achievement, and at the same time, to be loyal, even sacrificial, for the family (Nye 1976). "Look out for Number One; if I don't, nobody else will!" "Family life is the moral bedrock of the good life, we need to work at making it strong!"

Involvement in family throughout life means that members experience the loss of deep identities and the reversal of relationships of power and dependency between parents and children (Weigert and Hastings 1977). Dramatic plots of sons' ambivalence toward fathers can be interpreted more structurally as a general effect of family relationships and their contradictory developments: we begin as totally dependent children; develop into autonomous adults with still independent parents; and go on to become independent older adults with increasingly dependent parents as they live the longer lives that modern society brings for the time being. Eventually we realize that a long life brings us to a state of dependency once again. Tears at weddings manifest the bittersweet joy-sorrow at the transformation of a son or daughter into someone else's husband or wife. Family dreams mask contradictory social norms, and the resulting contradictory emotions are, at times, deeply troublesome in the face of actual events. Freud was right: living in a family generates ambivalence. Family life intensifies that contradictory identity of living an oxymoron, of being an "individual member" of any group.

## D. Interaction

Interaction and interpersonal relationships are the building blocks of social life. Here, too, we find generic contradictions. Building on Georg Simmel's work, Lewis Coser (1964) argues that contradictory tendencies toward both uniting and dividing persons are not an anomaly; they are actually essential to interactive relationships. After all, we are, as the Ancients knew, both angel and beast, mind and flesh, rider and horse. Although we typically define the flow of feelings as though they were single, real, and separable emotions like love, fear, anger, and so on, Coser appropriately quotes Simmel to the effect that, "What the observer or the participant himself divides into two intermingling trends may in reality be only one" (1964: 60). Following Freud and perhaps Merton, Coser generalizes Simmel's perspective:

> Close social relationships, characterized as they are by
> frequent interaction and involving the total personality of
> the participants, may be said to include in their motiva-
> tional structure an essential *ambivalence* in that they
> contain both positive and negative cathexes inextricably
> intertwined (1964: 64–5; italics added).

In analogous fashion, Jacqueline Wiseman recognizes
the importance of ambivalence in her preliminary theory of
sexual interaction (1976: 12; 241). The heart of the issue
seems to be the perennial tension between the potentially
contradictory feelings of sex and/or commitment, lust
and/or love: the classical dilemma of eros and agape. In general, interactional ambivalence is most intense if the total
person is involved and the time frame covers significantly
long periods of participants' lives. Perhaps the key tension
is long-term commitment versus immediate stimulation. It
is plausible to theorize that such tension is intensified within a mobile and individualistic culture that places the dilemma of personal autonomy versus group solidarity at the
forefront of consciousness and puts pressure on persons to
keep climbing a success ladder.

## E. Individual

At the individual level of analysis, stigma, that is, a
personal attribute defined as an instance of a negative
stereotype, alienates the person from that aspect of self's
total identity (Goffman 1963). Erving Goffman argues that
identity alienation generates ambivalent feelings about
one's own self within the stigmatized person. His analysis of
stigmas of body, group, class, and ethnicity apply to everyone to the extent that the person lacks positive attributes
or possesses negative ones. All of us, for all or part of our
lives, are faced with the immediate task of managing stigmas that are part of our identities.

In a male-dominated culture, for example, women are
likely to be somewhat self-alienated and to experience gen-
der-linked ambivalence (Bardwick and Douvan 1971). A cultural reason is that the relative lack of highly valued social

goals for women in a male-dominated society leads women to seek self-validation more in individual relationships than in socially recognized achievement. Furthermore, the female, especially at adolescence, experiences the body as both a desirable and dangerous, a powerful and debilitating cultural reality. Women ambivalently realize that they value qualities particular to females while they know that these same qualities are less important culturally.

Contradictory messages are part of female socialization in American society. Girls are taught, for example, to strive and achieve, but not beyond what is appropriate, nor in areas not accepted as proper, nor to expect the same support, understanding, or rewards. They may strive to achieve what is appropriate "for a girl," and this is likely to be less that what is appropriate for a boy. Rubin (1981: 49) notes that "such parental and social ambivalence leaves its mark, producing women who are cleft in two—torn between the intellectual and intuitive parts of self, between the need to achieve in the larger world and the need for human relatedness. . . . " These clefts leave achieving women with "two selves," one for the world of work and a partially contradictory one for the world of family. It is interesting to speculate that identity ambivalence of this kind is experienced more deeply by women than by men because of early family experiences, so that, if male gender roles change to include stronger expectations for familial behavior such as nurturant child care, we would expect increasing ambivalence within male identities as well.

Identity ambivalence of another kind is experienced by traditional religious persons living in the midst of an unbelieving and pluralistic culture. In his study of Orthodox Jews, Heilman (1977: 228) argues that ambivalence is evident in the "conflicting conceptualizations of a single status" that members feel when they try to make sense out of themselves and their surroundings. Those who consider themselves as "modern" experience a contradiction between their intended private identity and their apparent public identity. By contrast, Orthodox Jews who consider themselves "traditional" experience private identity and public identity as coherently the same. "Modern Orthodox Jews" realize ambivalence in the conflict they feel between self-definitions and public identities.

Up to now, sociological ambivalence has been referring to structural contradictions and the contradictory feelings that result from them. The task has been mainly descriptive and suggestive. Furthermore, I assume that ambivalence is, or eventually comes to be perceived as, a painful condition that motivates individuals to search for relief. The next question comes readily to mind: how do persons respond to ambivalence; what are the ways of "doing" ambivalence; what is illuminated about modern life by conceptualizing ambivalence as an independent variable, as a "cause," in the easy sense of this difficult term?

## *Responses to Sociological Ambivalence*

Individuals or groups who have built-in conflicts of interest, but who must also continue working or living together may try to handle this ambivalent relationship by making jokes about each other. The joke bites, but all relax with a laugh. Lewis Coser (1964) cites anthropological research suggesting that the ambivalent feelings of sons and mothers-in-law or competing clans give rise to systematic joking relationships that help discharge the hostility without wasting the relationship. Ruth Coser (1966) interprets humor among medical professionals performing surgery, and clowning among young boys or adolescent girls as functional ways of handling conflict and sustaining conflictual roles while working toward a common goal. In addition, when people are promoted to a higher status, humor can ease the mixed feelings about the security and friendships left behind as well as about the uncertainties that lie ahead. In a more serious area, Ruth Coser (1976: 556–76) argues that ambivalent authority patterns in the middle class family, in addition to psychological characteristics, helps explain the genesis of schizophrenic children. "Problems in living" or "mental illness" may be another domain of response to an ambivalence that is too intense or strategic for victims to handle.

In a cross-cultural study, Slater and Slater (1965) present support for the thesis that societies characterized by greater social distance between males and females and greater male power over females inclines mothers to feel ambivalence toward male children. Ambivalent mothers communicate their mixed emotions to male children through actions that are now supportive, now rejecting. The Slaters go on to argue that such ambivalent maternal relationships tend to generate sons who experience high personal achievement needs and who fear women. As a result, these sons would be highly ambitious and show narcissistic characteristics such as exaggerated displays of self and over sensitivity to criticism. It would be fruitful to apply this account to the dynamics that allegedly underlie the "culture of narcissism" in the United States today (cf. Lasch 1979; Rieff 1966; Sennett 1978).

Experimental psychologists offer different but suggestive data on responses to ambivalence. Katz and associates (1981) provide some evidence for what we may call an "ambivalence-amplification" hypothesis, building on speculative phenomena such as the super-committed convert. Katz finds that extreme responses to certain stigmatized persons may be related more strongly to ambivalent attitudes or feelings toward the target population than to positive or negative feelings. Experimental subjects with ambivalent attitudes toward black "victims" gave more negative responses than subjects with mainly positive or even negative attitudes. Other findings (Katz et al. 1977) partially corroborate the thesis that ambivalence is a painful condition and that it may lead to over-reactions, perhaps by increasing guilt or self-doubt that then needs to be overcome by excessively firm action.

Ambivalence can be functional or dysfunctional for social institutions, but in either case, it appears to be painful for the individual and to motivate a search for relief. The pain may lead to amplified responses in an effort to convince self that one of the two faces of ambivalence is the only valid and true self (cf. Katz 1981: 112fn). Such empirical analyses suggest the usefulness of ambivalence as an explanatory variable (see Room 1976, for a negative case).

## A General Model of Ambivalence

I would like to summarize the discussion by offering a model that builds on and tries to go beyond the work of Robert Merton (see Figure 1). The general model incorporates structural conditions that result in the commingled feelings of do-don't; attraction-repulsion; love-hate; etc. Merton and followers locate core sociological ambivalence in contradictory norms within a single role and status. The general model goes further in suggesting that ambivalence is generated by value and cultural contradictions that are more fundamental than and complementary to social structural sources. Contradictions stemming from the passage of time, incomplete knowledge, and the fusion of antithetical interpretations throughout life, plant the seeds of existential ambivalence within every situation.

A primary task of culture, then, is to translate these dual and divergent pressures into meaningfully defined single emotions consistent with the demands of social order and personal decisions. Here, again, is the central paradox: culture enables us to "do" existential ambivalence in order that we may act meaningfully, and yet any historical culture is only partly successful. Indeed, modern culture may now be raising the ambivalence quotient by generating secondary or sociological ambivalence through its own contradictions. Culture was the solution; it is now part of the problem. If there is any merit to this observation, then to feel ambivalence is not to be sick, it is to be quintessentially modern.

From the general model of incompatible expectations, definitions, and feelings, contradictions appear at different levels, e.g., within culture: tradition vs. reason; within status sets: wife vs. doctor; within a single status: doctor as business person vs. healer; within a single role: doctor healer as

# Figure 1
## A Generalized Model of Sociological Ambivalence

| The Human Condition | Structural Cultural Contradictions | Situational Contradictions | Self Contradictions | Responses |
|---|---|---|---|---|
| Life and Death; | Meaning vs. Absurdity; | Active-Passive; | Fate-Freedom; | Natural Attitude; |
| Society and Nature; | Means-Ends; | Instrumental-Expressive; | I-Me; | Ideology; |
| Culture and Self; | Multiple Status Sets, e.g., woman as doctor and wife; | Role Conflict and/or Inconsistency in Single Status, e.g., doctor as healer and business person. | Private-Public; Norm-Counternorm; Contradictory Expectations in Single Role, e.g., concern detachment; | Therapy; Communal Life; "Doing Ambivalence" e.g., codes of ethics, joking, humor, counter-cultures, mental illness, avoidance; |
| Complex, Individualized, and Rationalized Society, e.g., USA | Professions, Bureaucracy, Service Occupations | | Detached loyalty; | |
| | | | Biased Disinterest among doctors, bureaucrats, and scientists. | Typical Univalent Emotions; Exaggerated Attitudes or Behaviors; Denigrating Victims; Eschatologies. |

concerned vs. detached; and within self interacting with other: trusting vs. distrusting, or sincere vs. feigning.

Ambivalence is a debilitating emotional condition for the individual. It is a triumph of social order that societies so motivate meaningful action and offer interpretations of experience that ambivalence is typically defined as unusual, temporary, or finally, a personality shortcoming rooted in individual failure. From a sociological view of ambivalence, explanations that end in appeals to the inexplicable or to individual characteristics are a failure of analytic nerve, an unwarranted reductionism, or blaming the victim.

### Toward a Social Psychology of Ambivalence: Linking Structure and Emotion

The discussion thus far presents a preliminary codification of selective sociological and psychological writings on ambivalence and a general model. In this section, a tougher issue arises: taking steps toward a social psychology of ambivalence that links the discussion with emerging work in the sociology of emotions. The effort is preliminary and tentative. It relies mainly on Arlie Hochschild's "new social theory" of emotions (1983: 218–33).

In brief outline, Hochschild's theory derives from the imperatives of social action. Emotion is the experience of the sentient actor's organic preparation for action, not merely of the cognitive or decisional preparation. In an irreducible and immediate way, emotions are bodily as well as social signals, that is, organic sources of anticipation for what is happening next in the interactive world. They are a form of intentionality, of being-toward-action. Emotions focus a person's attitude, the internal organization of the body for action, by some kind of affective comparison with prior attitudes.

In Hochschild's terms, emotion emerges from "realities newly grasped." This new realization is sentiently projected over "the template of prior expectations." This template of prior attitudes forms an "assumptive base line" on which the self projects action into the future. The assumptive base line need not be only cognitive. Indeed, it hardly if ever is only cognitive. In the social psychology of emotion, it is taken to be sentient, organic, felt. In contrast to what we may call "symboling," emotions prepare what is coming next through the essential commingling of the body and intentions in physical signs (cf. Scheff 1973; Weigert 1983). In sum, emotions are signals based on comparisons forged on the embodied template of prior expectations behaviorally built into attitudes.

As signals for action-to-come-next projected by the situationally sentient person, these processes make up the preparatory stages of the social act. As we recall, George H. Mead took the social act as his basic unit of analysis for understanding human life. He unpacked the act into four stages: impulse, perception, manipulation, and consummation. The signal function of emotion readies the body for action (impulse) and anticipates what is coming next by comparison with prior bodily expectations. What renders emotions so powerful and irreducible to cognition is that they relate to the experiential aspect of self immediately, that is, with no intended cognitive mediation here and now. They are primitive or habitual and irreducible self-feelings entering into the constitution of social acts (Denzin, 1984). Such templates sometimes conflict with other modes of intentionality. We feel like doing one thing while simultaneously considering the thought that we ought to be doing something else.

Since emotions and accompanying sensations select and announce courses of action, persons must examine the selectivity of emotions and their interpretations. Interpretations are made available to us and expressed through the names by which we learn to identify emotions. Through socially available vocabularies, actors come to isolate and recognize experiences as separate emotions (Geertz 1959). As we name and know an emotion, a particular aspect of the total situation is abstracted out for selectively attentive focus. The adolescent girl defines what she feels as love and dreams of loving her knight accordingly; her parents define it as youthful infatuation and plan to act accordingly in the same feeling situation. For social action, a rose is not a rose by any other name. In other words, persons symbolically transform bodily attitudes into known expectations about how these sentiently selected and abstracted foci change what is signaled here and now. This inclination stems from the assumptive base line for action: self-understanding relative to the situation.

Hochschild (1983: 230) posits five categories of selectivity: what I want; what I have; what I approve; who is the causal agent; and what is the relation of self to the causal agent. A primary emotional experience relates self to each of these aspects of the situation. What Hochschild does not consider is the possibility that the self can experience two or more sentient attitudes or emotions in the situation, just as there may be a plurality of cognitive interpretations vying for dominance.

Imagine the situation of a traditional husband acting within the framework of romantic love trying to interpret the autonomy of a suddenly feminist wife. He thinks of himself as more powerful and correct, and so he feels angry with her. Simultaneously, he thinks of himself as committed to her happiness and support, and so he feels guilty about his anger. As a self struggling with two signals for guiding action, he cannot rely on feelings as a guide for acting correctly in the situation. In fact, his emotional predicament becomes part of the problem with the relationship to his wife.

The traditional husband's emotional dilemma is likely reflected in an inner struggle the wife experiences. Both struggles are instances of the contradiction between self versus group goals. As a result, the husband and wife do not know what each self wants; do not know what each self has vis a vis the other; do not know what actions to approve; do not feel in control of self or situation; and finally, do not know how to relate to each other. As a result, they do not know what to think, feel, or do here and now. Neither can identify with or feel self or other in an unambivalent way.

Ambivalence emerges from separately selected and contradictory aspects of situations experienced simultaneously. As such, it serves a further signal function that indicates a breakdown or "fracture" in the construction of the social act by splitting the process of comparison with prior expectations and the assumptive base line of self-understanding. Applying Hochschild's scheme to situational contradictions allows analysis of the genesis of ambivalent experience from simultaneous simple emotions. Such situational contradictions can be traced to structural and cultural contradictions. These traces link the experience of ambivalence to features of social organization, that is, they relate the general model of sociological ambivalence to a social psychology of ambivalence.

In terms of linking the ambivalent self-in-situation and contradictions in social organization, ambivalence can be defined as the experience of mutually blocking foci from two or more discretely defined emotions. The experience may be interpreted as confusion, indecisiveness, abulia, or ambiguity, but underlying the experience would be a fracture in the signal function of simple sentient emotions. As a result, the self senses a blunted or ineffectual emotional experience. There is no sentient or attitudinal focus to guide action. The person would not know what is being felt in the confused commingling of desire, guilt, fear, etc. Ambivalence triumphs. With modernity came a definition and label for this experience: we now have another "emotion" characteristic of our time.

With the breakdown in the typical signal function of emotion, the individual is unable to render a clear identification "of" or "with" self or the other. The process of "personification" or person-construction breaks down with regard to self and other (cf. Stone and Farberman 1981). To feel authentic in relationship to others and to self, individuals need guidance from emotions that feel credible and relevant to the situation. A situational breakdown in the routine "natural" signal function of emotions still signals a meaning; namely, a distressful fracture in the everyday sense of self as natural, at home in the world, and authentic. Ambivalence threatens that precarious and precious dramatic creation: the sense of a taken-for-granted ontology of self as authentically real. The "ontologized self" is essentially felt within the natural attitude that underwrites our assumed sense of normality.

## Summary

Part of the argument thus far derives from a sociology of knowledge axiom: concepts emerge when they are needed to make sense out of current situations. The rapidity, complexity, precariousness, and intensity of today's world are likely to generate increasing burdens of ambivalence, as Freud saw and we think the founders of sociology adumbrated. Building on developing work in the sociology of emotions, it appears that increasing ambivalence leads to blunting of emotional experience; threats to unquestioned self-identity; challenges to secure self-esteem; conflicting courses for meaningful social action; and in general, a threat to traditional ways of building a secure and satisfactory life. Enlightened understanding of the dynamics of ambivalence becomes, then, a necessary part of a genuine education that prepares moderns to live meaningfully now. And we must succeed, else we humans will be unworthy even of Buridan's ass. Following chapters pursue the Buridan predicament into considerations of individual, family, and religion, to put a bit of flesh on these theoretical bones, still more promissory than profound.

# Chapter 3

□

# The Sundered Self

Whatever else a human person is, it is a sentient animal—but not only that. And here, marked by the earliest artifacts buried with our ancestors to accompany their shadowed selves, lies the rub. Animals sense, and so do we, in spite of heavy socio-cultural overlays. We also idealize our sensations through the many modes of intentionality: abstractions, delusions, dreams, desires, crass self-interests, and altruistic sacrifices.

There is a price to pay for such complexity, for the push-pull of feelings and idealizations. There is an awareness of division at the heart of the sundered self, or at the seat of a horse and rider perhaps, or where an angel touches an animal, or simply where I meet me. One angle on the angelic animal is through ambivalence generated by these layers of existence. In this chapter, individual existence is examined for contradictory and paradoxical imperatives that structure emotional life.

*Three Kinds of Experiential Ambivalence*

At least three kinds of experiential ambivalence arise from the distinction between feelings and emotions. The first involves a contradiction between two feelings that are experienced as impulses moving the person in different directions. We can feel simultaneous attraction and fear toward someone. The first feeling draws us closer to the attractive person; the second feeling drives us away from the repulsive other.

Note that I am forced to write about these feelings as though they were clearly defined, that is, as though they were emotions. There is no choice in the limits imposed by the discursive medium of print, unless I were to seek media such as paint, stone, dance, etc. Pre-definitional levels of affective experience face the inadequacies of discursive communication. The same difficulty exists in discussing the pre-definitional self, e.g., the I or personal experience. Rather than use denotational symbols like primes or sub-scripts to designate "raw" pre-definitional experience or meaningful post-definitional events, the reader has to make the proper judgment depending on the context. I will try to use "feeling" for affective experiences that are pre-definitional, and emotion for those that are defined.

The second kind of experiential ambivalence involves a feeling and an emotion. This experience combines a pre-definitional affective experience and a socially defined feeling, an emotion, toward the same object. A son or daughter, for example, may experience a vague and puzzling antipathy for a parent who is also dutifully loved. The total experience is difficult to manage since only part of it is defined and can be objectified in discursive communication, the common medium for working out feelings in interaction with others. While the emotion is discussed, however, the affective experience remains outside of available language, unless the person is creatively gifted, or is willing to adopt a view of ambivalence as the experience of contradictory feelings, one conscious, the other unconscious. We do not judge the construct of an "unconscious" feeling as relevant for a sociological perspective on ambivalence, although pre-definitional experience may function in an analogous way.

The co-existence of two contradictory emotions makes up the third kind of experiential ambivalence. The clash between two socially defined feelings, such as explicit anger toward a customer who must simultaneously be treated warmly and politely, generates the paradigmatic sociological instance of experiential ambivalence. Contradictory emotions are available through typical linguistic means at the disposal of the self. This level of ambivalence can more readily be recognized, labeled, and analyzed. The sources for each contradictory emotion can be identified, at least hypothetically, and if accurate, the possibility of remedy can be pursued. For example, it can be hypothesized that as long as hysterical female patients were unable to define their feelings in terms of the repressive patriarchial structures of the time, many would be unable to manage their ambivalence. With the shift in structures and the availability of social psychological concepts, women can now articulate their experience differently and make new sense out of their emotions. Female hysteria is no longer the issue as it was in nineteenth-century Europe.

All three kinds of experiential ambivalence may block effective action. Consequently, the individual must resolve ambivalence sufficiently to go on acting within the limits of normality. Failure to resolve it adequately leaves the ambivalent person mired in the anxiety that eventually accompanies it. Furthermore, ambivalence, as suggested earlier, is linked to abulia or indecision. The social imperative to decide and act makes ambivalence a threat to a satisfactory life. Contemporary realities of individual existence, the imperatives to interact significantly, and the socio-cultural contradictions of today's world are objective sources of ambivalence that are not reducible to personal adequacy or inadequacy. Let us look at some sources of individual ambivalence.

At the experiential level, ambivalence flows from two affective inclinations that signal and move the individual in two lines of behavior that cannot both be enacted. Again, discursive language is used to discuss experience that is analytically prior to linguistic transformation into cultural categories. At this pre-definitional moment, ambivalence is the experience of undefined "commingled feelings." An individual may feel ambivalent about self, other, environment, or any "object." By object, we refer to whatever reality is symbolically constructed within experience that includes a relationship with self. The relationship is constituted by commingled feelings that grasp the object, including self as object. The latter possibility is powerfully illustrated by the self-feelings of suicidists, of sundered "selves hating and killing selves," for example, self as depressed killing self as guilty, or self as remorseful killing self as sinner.

Commingled feelings can have self or any symbolically constructed object as their focus. Even if self is not the primary object of the feelings, it is part of the dynamic field that constitutes the ambivalent experience. It is necessarily "I" who am simultaneously drawn toward and repulsed by that person whom I both love and fear, whether self or other. Commingled feelings inclining the individual toward mutually exclusive behaviors, such as nurturance and destruction, generate a primitive kind of ambivalence. There are also commingled feelings that re-enforce the same behavior, like the joy and pride a parent feels after watching a son or daughter in the school pageant, and that leads to a relieved hug for the child. The present focus is on commingled contradictory feelings that signal contradictory behaviors, thus blocking effective action. This kind of primitive individual ambivalence is, furthermore, a pre-definitional reality, and lies just outside of, and a bit prior to the focus of this book. Recognizing its importance, I leave it to scholars working the relevant disciplines.

The second kind of individual ambivalence is constituted by the "conflated affect" resulting from the simultaneous experience of a feeling and an emotion. Like commingled feelings, conflated affect may move a person toward two or more mutually exclusive behaviors. There are likewise conflated affects that re-enforce complementary actions. Present concern remains with those that move in mutually exclusive paths. Perhaps the paradigmatic example is the son who dutifully loves his father even while he severely resents him to the point of feeling hate in the inadmissible corners of consciousness.

Contradictory conflated affect is akin to Freudian

ambivalence with the acceptable emotion of filial love as conscious while the inadmissible hate is in some sense unknown but at work. From the phenomenological base of emotion as self-feeling, however, there are no feelings that are not experienced by self. There is no phenomenon such as an unconscious self-feeling. There are self-feelings that the person may either deny to self and others, or be unable to define. Such self-feelings remain vague and diffuse stirrings that trouble one's peace of mind. I conceive of "unconscious" feelings as those that the self may be unable to label because there are no cultural symbols, or because of what they would tell about self.

The paradigmatic son, then, experiences feelings toward his father. The feelings remain undefined and unobjectified so that the dutiful son can go on filially loving his father while he wrestles with vague, unlabeled feelings that move him toward rebelling against or even destroying his father, or toward displacing the hatred in non-normal behavior. From a social phenomenology of emotions, conflated affect reflects the contradictory structure of interpersonal relations. If the sociologically ambivalent structure is typical of that society, the unlabeled self-feeling will likely be selected and defined. Once defined and labeled, it is transformed into an object for analysis and control, i.e., into a known emotion.

In the third kind of experiential ambivalence, the self labels, defines, and thus knows each of two "contradictory emotions." Each emotion signals a mutually exclusive course of action; and verifiable institutional imperatives generate each of the contradictory emotions. Contradictory emotions explicitly link individual experience and social structure. They make a total social fact defined by the dominant institutional arrangements of society while they are simultaneously experienced as painful personal emotions. As a total social fact bringing together personal experience and institutional arrangements in a single phenomenon, individual/sociological ambivalence points to the paradox stated in chapter 1: culture functions to resolve primitive ambivalence, but modern culture generates secondary ambivalence that may be functional for society but disfunctional for the individual. The antinomies of human nature, subjective life versus objective form, are embodied, as it were, by the individual person struggling for meaning in the midst of modern culture (cf. Simmel 1950: 58 and passim). Ambivalence is at the heart of modern life.

### Interactional Ambivalence: What Do You Mean? What Do I Feel? How Do I Look?

Individual experience is one domain of ambivalence. Besides experiencing, however, all of us act. Indeed, it is more adequate to think of interaction, that is, the mutual enacting of social relationships. Although interaction is more than communication, since it results in objective outcomes affecting others and the environment, this section is limited to communicative aspects: what is intended; what is expressed; what interpretations are made by self and other; are they at odds with each other; and what does self intend versus what does self judge to have been expressed.

Some communicative results of interaction have become powerful concepts as well as widespread folk understandings. For example, there is the "self-fulfilling prophecy" formulated by Robert Merton, and the earlier idea by W. I. Thomas of the "definition of the situation." Briefly put, the definition of the situation helps us realize the objectifying power of ideas, namely, if persons define a situation as real, then it has real consequences regardless of the accuracy of the definition, since, accurate or inaccurate, it guides action.

The self-fulfilling prophecy is a future projection of that idea, namely, if persons believe that something is going to happen and act on those beliefs, the cumulative effect may well bring about that very happening. Beliefs lead to outcomes that would never have happened if individuals did not have those beliefs. Beliefs birth the event and become prophesies. If enough people believe that their votes do not make any difference, and as a result many individuals in that category do not vote, their prophecy becomes real, but not for reasons that they believe. I want to emphasize this point, because it touches on a major paradox in large-scale contemporary society. The fact is that my individual action qua individual makes an unnoticable or trivial difference, that is, virtually no difference at all. Yet, given the kind of society in which I live, and the life chances, fate, and ideology I share with others, my actions in conjunction with theirs bring about the very outcome that I seek to avoid. We may call this modern pathos to go with modern ambivalence.

An idea underlying modern pathos comes from psychiatrists concerned with effective communication. Watzlawick et al. (1967) formulated the "double-bind" problem. It directly relates to human intimacy and mutual understanding by analyzing contradictory messages and identities. To construct meanings for underwriting a satisfying life, a person must work through contradictory messages. Furthermore, the double bind is a social source of ambivalance.

Here is the double-bind at work (cf. Watzlawick et al. 1967: 211–2). Think of two or more persons involved in intense relationships situated in a shared context. One person communicates with the other. The message appears simple, e.g., "I love you," said by a father to his daughter. Analysis of the performance of the communication finds the message much more complicated, however. Watzlawick and colleagues see the following components in a double-bind message. First, there is the simple surface object that is communicated, love from a father to his daughter. Second, there is an assertion about the very object that is asserted in the simple message. This is a "metacommunication," that is, a communication about that which was simply communicated.

Metacommunication is often carried by non-semantic cues like body language or paralanguage such as pitch, tone of voice, etc. Erving Goffman (1959) speaks of the expressions we "give," that is, the simple semantic messages, and those we "give off," that is, everything else we communicate by the range of our appearances, from body odors to voice volume and gestures. If that father, for example, shrilly shouts the words with a tensed and aggressive body, while shaking his fist in his daughter's face, then the metacommunication says, "I control you and I demand that you be an extension of me." This metamessage contradicts the simple assertion of love.

The third aspect of a double-bind communication is that the simple message be contradicted by the metamessage: the tone of voice negates the simple message of love. The recipient and sender of the simple message must then violate the surface meaning in order to understand the total complex of messages that are sent. Most important, there is no way to know what single message is sent for the simple reason that no one message was ever sent. Two message levels, at least, were commingled in the total communication, and each may have more than one meaning, especially messages given off. The recipient and perhaps the sender is likely to respond to the communication with ambiguity and ambivalence. The communication embodies structured contradiction.

The communication breakdown and the emotional costs are compounded if the persons cannot step outside the contextual framework within which the messages occur. Given the tight context of power and intimacy in family life, perhaps neither sender nor recipient can legitimately comment about the metamessage, nor can either withdraw easily from the context of the relationship. Yet, the contradictory messages define future courses of action. Both parties, then, must try to respond to a logically meaningless but pragmatically imperative and self-denying message. In such a self-denying communication, the necessary trust underwriting interpretations of each other's message cannot be sustained (cf. Lewis and Weigert 1985; 1985a). Future action is likely to fall out along lines of power. Along the power lines lies the threat of punishment for failure to obey. The recipient is victimized.

If the recipient, for example, is in a subordinate power position, she is often prohibited from, or may be incapable of, showing any awareness of the logical and pragmatic contradictions in the message, and yet she must act in response to it. Consider such messages as: Be spontaneous; Don't be a conformist; Grow up and act your age; or, Don't stop loving me. These messages, if sent with imperative metalanguage cues, are self-contradictory as total communications. How can a recipient respond; what is to be decided, felt, done? Yet, the recipient fears that if she does not act rightly, she will be punished. But what or who is right?

The quandary of a double-bind communication produces varying results. Some find it a cause of schizophrenia (Coser 1976; Laing 1971; Watzlawick et. al. 1967). A common point in these analyses is that the message can split the recipient's sense of personal identity, as R. D. Laing put it, into a "divided self." From a sociological perspective, the Catch 22 nature of the communication is a feature of modernity. Indeed, Georg Simmel's turn-of-the-century writings about the antinomy between life and form, or the paradox of subjective and objective culture, captures the issue here pursued along its affective dimension.

The double-bind message as the exemplar of a contradictory imperative in social interaction suggests a variety of analogous contradictions. There is an analogy between the double-bind message and the double-bind status, the former referring to communication, the latter to social structure. Similarly, whereas others note the cumulative outcome of a self-fulfilling prophecy, consider its potential negative power by thinking of a self-denying prophecy. Self-denying prophecy would be characteristic of double-bind situations, both messages and statuses. Further, "self" has a dual meaning in the phrase; it refers to the identity content of the prophecy and to the existential person. Following the lead of therapeutically inclined analysts, double-bind situations lead not only to action that contradicts the literal semantic meanings of what is said, but also to action that destroys the recipient's sense of unified and authentic selfhood.

An instance of double-bind messages and statuses was given above in the discussion of the deep acting demanded of airline attendants. They had to present self according to the institutional norms of their work status even as they felt themselves repulsed according to the interactional norms of mutual respect and authenticity. Increasing demands for emotional labor to produce positive emotional service imply that double-bind statuses will become the fate of more employees, especially women.

A strong instance of double-bind status is that of sub-ordinate minority selves who need to interact with domi-nant majority others (cf. Dench 1986). Modern nation-states proclaim two contradictory principles: a universalistic egal-itarian norm inclusive of all citizens; and a particularistic elitist norm restricted to dominant strata. In response, the identity and motivation of minorities are divided between embracing universalistic citizenship and one's particularis-tic group identity. Here is how W. E. B. Du Bois put the con-tradiction early in this century: "One ever feels his two-ness,—an American, a Negro; . . . two warring ideals in one dark body, whose dogged strength alone keeps it from being torn asunder. The history of the American Negro is the his-tory of this strife—this longing to attain self-conscious man-hood, to merge his double self into a better and truer self. In this merging he wishes neither of the older selves to be lost" (1904: 3–4). Similarly, Ralph Ellison has a nameless and interactionally invisible protagonist reflect on his self-negat-ing links with others. Arguing with himself whether to leave the security of his dark cellar of escape from the world, the Black man reflects on his life of saying Yes while feeling No. "So I became ill of affirmation, of saying 'yes' against the nay-saying of my stomach. . . . I am an *invisible* man" (1953: 496, his italics). The anti-hero evokes the dramaturgical principle that each of us, at some point of self-understand-ing, is alienated from other and thus from the part of self that other defines. Ellison ends the novel with the call, "Who knows but that, on the lower frequencies, I speak for you?" (503). And for me.

A minority group identity known through appearances may not be subject to personal choice. What is usually meant by race or ethnicity is a powerful case of a divided self or structured contradiction based on a socially defined stigma. We expect some kind of ambivalence to follow from the assumption that the minority group has a living tradition of beliefs, rituals, and other membership criteria that can be attributed to the individual who "looks like" he or she belongs to that group. Appearances become the essence (on the fatefulness of appearances, see Goffman 1959; Stone 1962; Weigert 1983). Furthermore, this group exists in some tension with the dominant culture. This tension is visibly performed by the public etiquette of prejudice or the hidden costs of discrimination on the basis of criteria irrelevant to the tasks at hand.

Of necessity, minority-majority group relationships include links of subordination-dominance, of A with power over B. Also, the goals of the dominant group and the interests of the subordinate group are to some degree contradictory, at least in the short run, unless the unhistorical assumption is made that the majority will voluntarily cede privilege, wealth, or the priority of life's chances to the minority group. What happens if minority groups seek increased access to the reward structures? The strata benefiting from the current social arrangements will be most interested in reproducing privileges that gave them power to be handed on to their children. The struggle is fiercely joined at the margin of the lowest strata of the dominant classes and the front line of the minority group: lower middle class dominants, for example, often struggle with minority groups seeking improved housing, jobs, or schooling, while the ensconced privileged classes reside in garrisoned suburbs, private schools, and certificated professions.

To put the issue a bit crudely, the ruling class is interested in an adequate and relatively cheap lower class. Ruling elites favor steps to keep a minority group at a legal, educational, and occupational distance. At the same time, the lower margin of the dominant society is interested in denying minority groups access to privilege, not because they wish to exploit them, for they are in no position to do so, but merely because they perceive, and this perception is re-enforced by ruling class media, that the minority is a threat to the marginal majority's precarious socio-economic security. To this effect, the dominant classes may, sotto voce, foster the usual racial and sexist myths that reenforce the ideology of denying equal access to minority types, whether black, brown, female, yellow, religious or whatever. Presidential campaigns are occasions when such myths are given tactical play in TV ads.

The overt, and more insidiously, the covert conflict between the official rhetoric of the dominant strata and the empirically available life chances for large numbers of minority persons creates contradictions between minority membership and the presumptively superior majority identity and between individual and group identities. If the minority person strives to succeed in terms of the norms and identities of the dominant group, she or he must, in some sense, deny those self-feelings and identities that are specific to the minority group. The minority group identity of "we" is negated by donning as much of "their" identity as the minority's appearance and skills allow. If the donning fails, the minority person becomes a kind of free-floating "I" that belongs to no group by ascriptive criteria but goes it alone by whatever path is open.

The minority person striving to make it in the majority world faces imperatives such as "Don't be a typical Hispanic American; be successful," or perhaps, "Be a successful (Hispanic) American." Similar imperatives would be put to Black Americans, or, in an interesting reversal of adjective and noun, to American Indians. These imperatives are analogous to the double-bind communication that accompanies the double-bind status. At the level of the object, the minority person is told to be what you empirically are, i.e., Hispanic and American. At first glance, this seems a reasonable imperative; there are Hispanic Americans who succeed. Depending on the situation, however, the imperative could be a contradiction for a rural, uneducated, non-English speaking barrio child. This child simply cannot follow the imperative with any plausibility. He or she is divided by a system in which success is too unlikely and escape too costly.

For others, such as Hispanic Americans who are truly bicultural and bilingual with a good chance to succeed in the dominant professional or business world, the imperative begins to take on the double-bind quality of a paradox: it commands action and identity that appear to be reasonable, achievable, and indeed, ideal, namely, be a successful hispanic American, with a lower case "h." For many Hispanic Americans, however, the imperative makes a self-reflexive assertion about itself. The metamessage, that is, the meaning that the imperative communicates about itself, is paradoxical: it asserts that, in order to succeed, the Hispanic American must become an hispanic American, in short, cease being an Hispanic at heart, become an American only, and succeed to the extent that skill, structure, and luck allow. To fulfill the total meaning of the imperative, the person must disobey the everyday meaning of the command, and in fact cease to be what it affirms, namely, American, successful, *and* Hispanic. Taken as a total social fact in a single imperative, it is contradictory and cannot be fulfilled.

This double-bind analysis clarifies the structured identity crisis with which bicultural minorities struggle throughout their lives, or at least up to that point at which they renounce one of the conflicting identities. To the extent that the minority identity is tied into bodily appearances or primary socialization patterns that are difficult or impossible to change, the identity is difficult or impossible to doff. Ethnic identities are not merely relational constructs; they are also sticky and fateful appearances. They often have a primordial quality. Until the paradox is broken and the contradictory identity structure is resolved, the minority person is likely to feel ambivalence both in public and imagined presentations of self. Consequently, effective action is difficult and the probability of extreme responses increases.

Linguistic "code switching" among Mexican-Americans illustrates the paradoxical and contradictory communication that at times characterizes relationships between dominant Anglos and bicultural and bilingual minorities. In the hands of Mexican-American poets, code switching communicates the dual meaning of the so-called "chicano" identity. The duality of identity is mirrored in the duality of languages, without even considering the semantic content of the words (Candelaria 1985). Consider the following poem

of a meeting between a representative of the dominant culture, an English-speaking bureaucrat, and a traditional
Spanish-speaking Mexican.

                    address
                address occupation
                age
                marital status
                –perdone . . .
                    yo me llamo pedro
                telephone
                height
                hobbies
                previous employers
                –perdone . . .
                    yo me llamo pedro
                pedro ortega
                zip code
                i.d. number
                classification
                rank
                –perdone mi padre era
                    el señor ortega
                    (a veces don jose)
                race

                              (Alurista 1971)

The dual structure and switching between English and
Spanish reflects the poet's understanding of the relationship between the carriers of the two cultures. The Anglo
Bureaucrat challenges with questions. The Hispanic client,
maybe a peasant-like Campesino, is four questions behind,
and quite respectful of the Bureaucrat. The Bureaucrat
starts with the business of filling in information. The
Campesino counters with a polite "perdone," or "pardon
me." Undeterred by the Campesino's polite (but perhaps
unintelligible to the English speaker) response, the Bureaucrat goes on questioning. After four more questions, the
Campesino is still back where he was, asking for pardon;
giving his name, "pedro"; hoping to please the Bureaucrat;

but lacking even the capital letter due to proper names. He adds his surname though it too lacks even the self-confidence of capital letters. He remains a most humble "pedro ortega." The Bureaucrat does not validate this personal identity; pedro is transformed into nothing more than a cifer in a category to be identified via answers to status questions.

The Campesino's efforts, respectful and humble, lack any clout. The Bureaucrat goes on asking four new and more difficult questions without an answer to any of the previous questions. What is the Campesino to do? He appeals to the next rule of identification that he knows, and presumably, that gets results in his own culture. He appeals to his genealogy, respectfully, "pardon me, my father was mister ortega." He adds, likely with a touch of pride, "sometimes, don jose," "don" being a title of respect for worthy elders. Again, pedro cannot say his name nor that of his father, even with the respectful title of "don" with capital letters. This is pedro's best shot, yet the Bureaucrat remains unmoved and starts into the next, and for the poet apparently most significant questions headed, and abruptly ended, by "race," a category the Bureaucrat could supply without asking, if he had eyes to see. Thus ends a cultural encounter rife with misunderstanding, but ripe for interpretation.

From the freedom of aesthetic distance the poet uses code switching as a device to capture the structural situation of dominant/subordinate cultural players. The poetic situation is analogous to society. Just as dominant/subordinate members re-enact the scripts reproducing the structure that gives them their identities, so the poet creates a poem within which both recite the lines that define them. The narratives within which such definitions exist make up the human reality of individual lives. Neither of the protagonists personally switches codes; each is locked in a self-defining code. The poet's license to switch codes provides the key for the reader to see that the protagonists are indeed trapped as players. It is the essence of art to transcend the limits of conventionally reproduced existence. It is the artist's cry inviting readers to become poets.

The poetic use of code switching illustrates the double-bind status of cultural minorities in relation to the dominant society. They are involved in contradictory structures, interactional situations, and experiential meanings. The presumption is that they would be likely to experience ambivalence as they try to act significantly both to pursue personal goals and to meet cultural imperatives. On a lower frequency, moderns must be poets skilled at code switching as they struggle to make sense out of situationss. There is a chicano, or better, chicana in each of us.

Analogous to the double status that defines ethnic minorities is the double status of women in what is still a patriarchal culture. Consider the imperative, "Be a successful woman!" What does the command say? If we define woman according to the cultural content of patriarchy, a woman is dependent on the male for name, status, support, protection, and fulfilment. Further, taking the less noble aspects of a patriarchal culture, a woman is seen as less important, less serious, intellectually short, irrationally emotional, and unfit for the really crucial tasks facing major institutions, especially the ruling and defense of the Nation. The bottom line is that women remain relatively powerless, both empirically and ideologically.

On the other hand, what does it mean to be "successful"? Without exaggerating, I could list the contradictory qualities to those listed in the preceding paragraph. Success is autonomy. It means to win status on your own, preferably through money. Certainly, it means to be taken seriously and considered important. Often these qualities are linked with decisive institutional positions dealing with power, above all else. Look at the gender composition of elites in government, business, education, religion, military, science, or any power-generating domain of American society. Christine Williams (1989: 79–80), for example, finds that women marines have mixed emotions toward a central part of themselves. They feel positive identification with their femininity and what it means to them. At the same time, they experience the disparagement of femininity in the

Marine Corps with which they also centrally identify. A woman marine is a stigmatized identity. Among their responses to this ambivalence, women individualize their situation by insisting that "I" can make the grade by being so good that I succeed anyway; or they turn the discrimination into a structural advantage by noting that negative bias leads to the selection of only the best women, so they are better, on the average, than the men.

To be a successful woman is to deal with a double-bind command that can be fulfilled only by denying what it says. The metamessage to women, as Lillian Rubin (1981) said, is to succeed, but not too much, not beyond what is proper for a "girl." To succeed really, one would have to cease to "be" a woman, according to typical cultural definitions. To succeed really, a woman must redefine what she is and does; she must enter a structure of experience that is ambivalent, if she had a typical patriarchial enculturation, that is, if she was raised to be a "proper" girl.

Arlie Hochschild (1983) argues that buying and selling human emotions in today's economy amplifies the estrangement of feelings from the self. As she writes, "... in the country that most publicly celebrates the individual, more people privately wonder, without tracing the question to its deepest social root: What do I really feel?" (198). This question is fraught with more than feeling; it signals a deep disruption in self-understanding. Feelings are foundational for selfhood because they tell us "the *self*-relevance of what we see, remember, or imagine" (196, her italics; see 85). Feelings signal in two directions: inwardly, they tell us who we are; and outwardly, they announce how we relate to self, others, and to the situation, and what we are likely to do next. To fulfill their signal function, feelings are socially defined, that is, transformed into emotions. When these emotions are traded as products of the business rather than exchanged as gifts of the person, however, persons become alienated from them just as from any other part of their labor that is taken over by those who buy and sell it. This emotional marketing most likely involves women. Although Hochschild does not make this conclusion, emotional labor

is likely to increase the laborer's ambivalence, both to self
and to the job.

Just as feelings internally signal the self-relevance of
the situation, appearances announce the situational relevance of our selves. Fred Davis (1985; 1987) formulates
what he calls "dialects of identity" that are signaled through
clothes and the trends of fashion. A basic dialect of identity
is gender, and within gender, there is the situational tension
of the erotic and chaste: look at me but see my clothes; look
at my clothes and see me—or that aspect of me that I want
seen in the way I want it seen. Clothes simultaneously cover
and expose the body, mask and announce the self, at times
both chaste and erotic.

Clothes signal *externally* the situational relevance of
self, and one of the dynamics underlying fashionable presentation is ambivalence. Davis begins with the dialectics of
"master" identities: gender, class, age, and status. The most
salient social objects toward which persons feel ambivalent
is likely to be their own selves (1987: 4). One source of evidence is the shifting erotic and chaste fashion codes
through which selves, and apparently with more historical
frequency, female selves, present themselves as simultaneously attracted by and withdrawing from sexual appearances. Davis suggests that "because these ambivalences
arise from structural tensions at the deepest moral reaches
of Western culture, they tend to be collective in character"
(1987: 14). As a collective reality, such ambivalences are
worked into the "fashion cycle" driven by cultural tensions.

A more speculative telling of cultural tensions is Ernest
Becker's psychoanalytic argument. In *The Denial of Death*
(1975), Becker argues that culture is a set of armour against
the reality of our animal existence and especially our mor-
tality. He captures this theme by characterizing culture as a
"vital lie" enabling humans to deny their body and
inevitable death. The denial serves as a necessary illusion
for constructing cultural meanings. It is as though humans
accepted a double-bind command along the lines of "live
fully." The command, however, includes a metamessage
requiring us to deny death by putting it outside of aware-

ness or defining it as an enemy of the life. Modern culture, as Phillippe Ariès and others have argued, fails to teach us how to die. Death is scientifically and medically denied as a threat and banished from our thoughts. The ban, of course, is doomed to fail. Besides, denying death denies life. At moments of crisis and solitude, death insistently drops by for a passing greeting. In spite of cell research and cryogenics, we know that death is our future. One visit is for keeps.

Becker argues that we fail to confront the premise of a healthy, full life; namely, "I know and accept that I will die." This admission is a first step toward heroism. Yet, we live the paradox of the denial, a so-called higher standard of materially living what is a psychologically dead life. We deny physical death in order to live the cultural commands of society, but in living by denial, we die psychologically and potentially. Heroism is crushed and courage is coopted by the cultural blandishments of the easy life. The truth, it turns out, is the reverse of cultural commands: in order to live fully, we must die to our culture and live the reality of our dying bodies. Not denial, but acceptance of death unleashes potential heroism. Cowardly clinging to our lives, we become cultural clones. Becker's is a psychoanalytically forged rendition of Jesus' paradoxical command to win life by losing it. To obey the message to live fully, we must deny its cultural meaning and break out of the context in which the message is given. Breaking out of one's culture is not easy, if possible at all, and Becker provides no formula. He ends with an exhortation to work for life to the fullest.

A more specific application of psychoanalytic reasoning is Robert Jay Lifton's struggle to come to terms with the nuclear context. The question is, How ought or do persons go on living "normal" lives with the knowledge that there are more than enough nuclear weapons to end human life as we know it? His work with survivors of the atomic blasts on Hiroshima and Nagasaki, Vietnam veterans, Nazi doctors, and nuclear scientists supports his assertion that the level of technological violence and psychological terror demands that psychic defenses be built around modern awareness. He calls the defense "psychic numbing" (cf. Lifton 1976;

1986; Lifton and Falk 1982). A totally terrorized organism cannot function. Moderns, if they think empirically about their situation, are likely to feel terror. The coping response of the organism is to disattend the terror. If the threat is still present, the terror unbearable, and the need to act imperative, then evolutionary wisdom numbs the organism so it can go on living.

Just as Simmel and Goffman noted that modern urbanites live normally amidst constant challenges and stimulation by becoming "blasè" or by "civil inattention" to the goings on, even murder; so too, Lifton finds that if the threat comes from our psychic interior, we can disattend even our own selves. We practice "psychic inattention." To be modern, then, is to be alienated from our innermost sensitivities about crucial matters such as nuclear terror or pollution of the life-support systems. This divided self is structurally homologous to the sense of ambivalence toward others. The ubiquity of double-bind situations appears to be characteristic of modernity. Even the sense of time comes divided.

### The Ambivalence of Time: Linear Circles

Whatever disagreements surround the understanding of time, analysts agree that it forms a foundation for experience and is an issue both individuals and societies must face. Solutions to the demands of time are necessarily temporary; time re-opens as an issue for each generation. The conventional division of time into past, present, and future is not as obvious nor as universal as normally thought. What is more to the point is that the experience of time concerns what is our responsibility and what is not. The past has already happened and is part of the empirical record, however that record is rewritten. The future is not yet. Are humans left with a present that is merely specious? Time is real; but the present is not; and the past was real; though the future is not yet. Part of the future is entrained in cycles of life by which our bodies run; the rest is played out in linear processes issuing from the minds and hands of human animals (Young 1988).

To be sure, history is re-written and experience is reinterpreted. There is no history beyond the reach of human activity, since history is a constructed account of the meaning of what is past. The past, as such, is gone, and remains part of the behavioral flow of events forever beyond human reconstruction. To the extent that we are animals, we have a past; to the extent that we are angels, we are timeless; to the extent that we are both animals and angels, we have histories that are never beyond retelling and reinterpretation.

The past we know to have been real and beyond recall as real. It is known only as remembered. The present, on the other hand, we think of as within our control, a convenient illusion generated by the structure of language and culture. As thinkers delight in pointing out, the present is an infinitesimal razor's edge, a specious will o' the wisp. Either a thing or event is, or it is not yet, or it is about to be. If it is, then it is now past and out of our grasp; if it is not yet, then it is future and not yet in our grasp.

The point is not to fall into philosophical antinomies, but to focus on the fact that the experience of time is divided into what persons can still decide and do versus what is already done. Of course, the past is further divided into many domains, in particular, into that which is retrievable and that which is forever past. My room may be colored a pasty cream, but that past can be redone by a new coat of paint. My father is dead, and nothing can undo that. My youth is wearied away, never to be re-awakened. So too, the present is divided into anticipations, expectations, half-done projects, barely kept promises, and final touch-ups, not to mention lies and illusions. The present is a process, whereas the past is a package and the future is a fantasy. Human futures live as some kind of future-projecting intentional grasp which we flex like fingers circling things and shaping events that are mere imaginings. The future emerging from the forces at work in nature and society is not likely to be the future held in our minds and even that is not likely to be the one held in our hands.

Both past and future are divided along lines that rend the human person into an animal and an angel. Parts of the person become parts of life living. Parts that were are long dead. Parts that are never will be. The past is divided into the irretrievable behavioral and physical flow of brutish events, and the forever retrieved historical meaning, for now, of the irretrievable. So, too, the future is cleft into that imagined state of affairs that lives in the projections of plans, predictions, wishes, and hopes, and the actually approaching state of affairs carried by physical or social forces triggered by human decisions and actions. The pathos of the future is that some parts contained in the pro-jected grasp of intentions does indeed come to be, but never quite as projected—ignorance alone sees to that. Other parts of the future are never foreseen, or if foreseen, carry with them new directions that lie outside the ken of our imaginings. Such irony is intrinsic to human action. More prosaically, social thinkers often overlook time by speaking merely of the "unintended consequences" of human action. Lovers swear fidelity only to end ironically in a bitter parting.

The unintended and unforeseen add pathos to what we do. There is yet an additional frame available to angelic humans, however. As noted above, there is the natural, but also the supernatural frame for making sense of what we do and the futures we imagine. Institutionally, the natural frame is exemplified by scientific worldviews with imagined futures based on empirically grounded methodologies, and with technological instrumentation for bringing about those futures. The supernatural frame, on the other hand, is typi-cally housed within religious institutions based on the range of faiths and transcendentally grounded worldviews, sometimes with social movements attached, though rarely with strong technological links.

For scientists, foretelling what the world will be in a designatable future is outside the methodological and evi-dential limits of their framework. They venture such projec-tions as concerned citizens or policy makers. For religionists, however, imagined futures are part and parcel of the total religious worldview formulated as an eschatology. Whatever their differences, Christians tend to agree that eschatology, or futures imagined according to God's revealed will, is central to Christianity (see Weigert 1988). During much of history, the scientific and the religious view of the end of the world, or end-time thinking, contradicted each other. Religionists held a strong option for an apocalyptic vision of falling stars, burning earth, and poisoned water, while scientists tended to the vision of progress through science, technology, and social engineering. Progress versus apocalypse were the options for imagining the future of society.

With the dawn of the twentieth century, however, came not only the critical voice of new social and psychological disciplines, but also the widening cataclysms that burned over and split the birthplaces of science and progress. World Wars I and II, topped by the advent of atomic bombs and the continual, violent conflicts of the post-war world exorcised the siren of progress. Additionally, the dawning awareness of systemic terrestrial pollution points to a future that is not a temporary hostage to international conflict, but a shadow of technological "progress" itself.

The transformation of progress into crisis has a major ironical result: previously opposed kinds of end-time thinking, religious eschatological apocalyptics and scientific projections, come to similar versions of a dire end if humans do not mend their ways (see Barkun 1983). Religionists predict the destruction of the world in great battles culminating in Armageddon; scientists teach the probabilities of nuclear holocaust and the possible destruction of mammalian life; environmentalists warn of pollution of the life-support systems, or of destruction of the life-protecting features of the earth like the ozone layer. Whether change can avert final disaster is a question for the religious ideology or the political optimism of the analyst. Progress can be read in current events along with its twin Regress. The basic meaning of time and decisiveness reveals modernity to be deeply Janus-faced.

If the circle we walk is large enough relative to our perceptual power, it appears as though we are walking a straight line. Striding along the arcs of a great circle, we may think we are moving ahead when in fact we have already

started back. Historically, individual life is like a tiny seg-
ment of a great arc that is a straight line in some temporal
aspects, like the organism's line from birth to death. Yet, a
culture's myths of history, cosmology, and end-time thinking may teach the individual that time truly is a circle. Religionists and scientists may begin to converge on the picture
of the end approaching, an end that is a beginning, an
eschatological entry into a transformed existence for the
religionist, and an evolutionary return through catastrophe
to earlier stages in the natural history of life for the scientist. With these diverging pictures based on similar readings
of the times, interpreted as portents or probabilities, come
split attitudes toward the split atom and the spliced gene.
These splits both symbolize and effect steps of progress
and signal portents and probabilities of a return to heaven
or a pre-mammalian earth.

Split attitudes reflecting the splitting of the environment's key operatives—atoms and genes—provide a deep
structural base for feeling ambivalence. Even more perva-
sively, the splitting of modern consciousness enters the
experience of the basic form of time, namely, the
sequencing of that which I can decide and effect, and that
which is done and which I can only redefine. The experience
of time, rather than resolving ambivalence from other
sources, now becomes another and deeper source of
ambivalence. Temporal ambivalence is an instance of the
leitmotif: modern culture generates ambivalence.

Translate temporal ambivalence into truths, that is,
propositions informing life. "Save for a rainy day," or "Play
now, pay later." "Save your soul forever by losing it now," or
"Eat, drink, and be merry, for tomorrow. . . . " "Death where is
thy victory?" or "Rage, rage against the dying of the light."
"Every day in every way, I get better and better," or "Aging is
a curse." Each statement tells us how to define our lives;
each pair is a contradiction of sorts; each is proclaimed by
one or another institution of modern society. No place,
except in a utopia, are they reconciled. To feel ambivalent
about today is to be modern. And so too is wondering
where tomorrow will be.

### *The Ambivalence of Space: Away to Here*

The duality of temporal reality has its analogue in the spatial realm in which we walk our appointed times. A cautionary tale can be told. A garbage barge dispatched from a hopeful community at the non-New York City end of Long Island searched down the East coast and off to foreign islands only to be told in clear language that its cargo was unwelcome. Garbage is not every port's favorite import, though some states pick up foreign exchange along with foreign waste.

Somehow, the failure of the garbage to go away from that hapless Long Island community, Islip, which had eventually to take it back, strikes us on first glance as not quite cricket. After all, we learned from childhood that all you do with garbage is "throw it away." There seems to be no ambiguity nor possibility of ambivalence in the old linear world in which waste was simply thrown away from oneself. Once something is thrown away, it is gone; and presumably gone for good, if not forever. If I throw something "away," it and I are not to be in the same place again. Where it goes, no one is quite sure. Now, after the Long Island garbage-barge affair, moderns cannot even be sure that it can be thrown away, ultimately.

In a collective and ecological sense, our common sense idea is totally wong. It is never possible to throw anything away. Short of shooting garbage beyond the farthest reaches of outer space where it would be outside any measurable system supporting our lives (and even this leaves it "in" our cosmos), whenever humans throw anything away, it comes back to them in the form of later generations' life changes carried in their life-support systems. The systems of air, water, food, energy, soil, and genes apparently are relatively closed. The turnaround time available for transforming spatial garbage into life-support space seems to be getting shorter with each generation. Shortening turnaround time suggests that traditional frames for making decisions concerning what I may call "garbage space" are no longer adequate. Linear thinking that throws garbage away into ground, air, or sea where we are not, has no validity.

Ground filling, incineration, or dumping at sea each has its risks to current and future generations' life-support space. Linear frameworks for thinking about garbage in which it goes away without returning are being replaced with circular models. Garbage is now a circular phenomenon; it is a boomerang. If humans throw it away, it comes back at some time in some form. The circle, not the line, is the metaphor of human-environment spatial interaction.

Yet, the combination of linear temporal and spatial thinking persists, if not in our reasoning, then in our actions. We continue throwing things away. Indeed, the disposable economy is widening its scope with throw-away cameras to go with throw-away bottles. Once again, modern consciousness is split. This instance is characterized by the split between what we know and how we model the workings of the world, and the way we live and how we model our own behavior. We go on living pretty much as we have been: producing, consuming, and throwing away, even as we become aware that we are "Fouling our own nests." This split in spatial awareness and behavioral links with the environment provides another source of ambivalence. The physical objects around us take on a kind of mystical dynamism; they are literally *in via,* on the move. As vitalists have argued, inert physical objects take on a kind of life if we learn to think of them as intimately related to our lives. Their "life" is a projection of our own mixed feelings.

## Utopia is Noplace: From Eternity to Here

The combination of my lifetime and this space makes it my place. Every person has a sense of place: where I am; where I was; where I am going. "Place" brings together our sense of time and space. It makes a single experience out of linear organic time as I flow from birth, through life, to death, and the indeterminate movements around the space available to me as I go here, there, and back again. Life is both linear and circular, but the duality is not so discernible as I decide and act in terms of one or the other. Ambivalence appears to deepen.

In a couplet of books, Yi-Fu Tuan presents materials illustrating ambivalence toward spaces become places. Ancients felt ambivalent toward the wilderness, a place of fearful unknowns like beasts and chimeras yet one attracting exploration and development. The social response was to build paradises, homes, gardens, and farms reflecting nature rearranged for the security and order of community. Yet, communal space is also constraining and weighed down with everyday routines. Individuals remain ambivalent to community and to its places. In the modern situation of global threat to long-term futures, humans have reversed their emotional response to the wilderness: what was once the unordered fearful place is now a fragile remainder of natural order threatened with destruction by the (dis)order of industrialized states. Thus, we remain ambivalent toward wilderness, but the emotional loading has switched. As Tuan notes, the human search for an ideal environment seems stretched between the antipodal images of a "garden of innocence and the cosmos" itself (1974: 248; see Nash 1976: xii, passim, for ambivalence in the American mind toward wilderness).

In a later book, Tuan finds ambivalence toward "landscapes of fear" (1979: 81; 113 ff; 189; 210; 216). He notes recurrent ambivalence as: medievals confront the forest; humans look upon and interact with dead homo sapiens; reformers consider a prison as both a place of punishment and rehabilitation; and, in general, humans face the push-pull of community that both secures and restricts. Self is drawn to and repelled by a world that is ordered and chaotic, beautiful and fearful, life giving and death dealing. Reality is both pure and dangerous. Societies are structured by the boundaries drawn around these zones and the consequences for those who are in the wrong place at the wrong time (cf. Douglas 1970). Mere movement in the cultured world can be an ambivalent experience.

Rene Dubos generalizes this line of thinking into "environmental ambivalence" (1980: 128 ff). Ancients typically saw wilderness as enticing and threatening. Moderns both recognize the virtues of intact wilderness and the need to preserve it, and resent changes in the inherited version of the scaped environments built over the centuries. The general response is fascination and fright, almost an echo of the numinous experience of the sacred. The contemporary context is doubly paradoxical: not only does it present moderns with conflicting emotional responses to the wild and tamed environments, but it raises other historical firsts in the recognition both of the possibility of wilderness extinction and of the need for modern rationalities to "manage the wilderness" lest it disappear. The contradictory implications of the phrase "managing wilderness" elicits mixed emotions in the knowing reader. Whatever ambivalences are elicited by the constructs of "management" and "wilderness" are compounded by their interweaving in the joint probabilities of human survival. The critical environmental issue remains: can management succeed in what nature has been doing up till now?

There are cultural responses that resolve ambivalence. Whether they would have any effect on the objective sources of the mixed emotions is a question for empirical analysis. As Karl Mannheim recounted fifty years ago in his book on ideology and utopia, these are two basic responses to the crisis of any age, especially our own. Persons can ideologically redefine events and forces at work in the world in terms of what they believe has been a privileged period in history. Believers hold a social formula preserved in the group's ideology.

The ideological formula is known, has worked, and need only be applied properly against those who do not believe or will not conform. Take the situation of the nuclear arms race and the possibility of nuclear holocaust. The life of the group is paramount; loyalty is the supreme and absolute virtue; strength is the necessary means; no sacrifice is too great, no risk is too costly; my Country, right or wrong, and it is always right for those who believe. This ideological stance absorbs ambivalence and leaves believers certain in their minds and secure in their hearts. It is the stance of the super patriots of the world, whether they believe in the US or the USSR.

The final ideological nail comes in the hands of those who believe not only that it is sweet and proper to die for one's country, *dulce et decorum est pro patria mori,* but also that it is justifiable to put the world's population and life support systems at risk. The ideological sweep that puts everyone under the carpet is the marvelous development of what is anachronistically called nuclear "warfare." Nuclear war is war only for ideologues who equate war with destruction of the enemy rather than the classical idea of a pragmatic extension of state policy by other means. Nuclear war fails to be war on two counts: it destroys not only the enemy but the earth and friends as well; and it carries out no policy of conquest for the commonweal.

What option is left for those who do not wish to be certain and secure ideologues? They can believe in some kind of utopia, a future state of community that has never been known, a transcendent turn to the human story. Belief in progress promised a scientific utopia for those fortunate enough to live in the advanced Western societies in which rationality became a secular religion. In opposition to capitalist supported science rose an alternate utopian promise of the classless society of total egalitarianism, an idea born of the centuries of Christian yearning symbolized in the Utopia of St. Thomas More and translated into the utopia of Marxism, the last hope, it seems, of those who dreamt of heaven on earth.

The utopian fecundity of Christianity gave birth to a more radical utopia, a paradise of an earth remade by Christ returning to govern a worldly heaven: the millenium of Christ's Kingdom on earth cleansed by the violence of Armageddon. The best-selling American book of the 1970s was Hal Lindsey's story of the destruction and transformation of the earth into God's Kingdom, *The Late Great Planet Earth.* Those who believe in this kind of a utopian finish have an answer to ambivalence: believe and be saved. The certainty is part of the saving action of God's grace and a sure sign that indeed you are saved. The formula may sound circular, but apparently it works for millions of Americans.

Finally, there is a secular version of the utopian quest that has its adherents. It is not quite this-or other-worldly. Nor is it mere science fiction. It is the last frontier, space travel. If the cosmonauts could not find God in outer space, then seekers have plenty of space for travel and colonization. Clearly, over five billion earthlings cannot mount space ships in even the most fictive projections. Space life, then, is a psychological escape for modern utopians, much as the western frontier may have worked in the collective psyche of nineteenth-century immigrants to America. Relatively few immigrants went west in wagons, but perhaps millions went there in dreams. So moderns may be homeward bound to distant Empires that strike and strike back in their dreams when the terror outside their apartments strikes at their heart.

*Summary*

Ambivalence lives within individual experience. There are the experiences of mixed feelings, a vague and diffuse sense of being pulled in two directions, a sense that defies clear statement because the experience includes unformulated feelings. Then there is the situation of feeling pushed or pulled, even though we have a defined and normal emotion pulling in a different direction, like the groom-to-be "knowing" for sure that he loves his wife-to-be. Indeed, he is able to avow to her and himself just that, even as he feels twinges of deeper opposing feelings that he is unable to express in words to himself, to her, or to anyone else for that matter. Finally, there is the situation of two defined feelings or contradictory emotions that push and pull a person toward mutually exclusive courses of decision and action. This is ambivalence in the strict sense.

Exploring sources of ambivalence, I focused on the structure of one kind of communication, namely, double-bind messages. These, in turn, reflect the situation of double-bind statuses that are a characteristic of modernity. A telling double-bind status is that of minorities struggling with two identities exemplified by a poet's code switching between English and Spanish. Although the language remains English, the status of women in the context of patriarchy has double-bind applications. Finally, the suggestions of Ernest Becker lead us to consider the human situation of living unto death as existentially ambivalent.

Death is but one of the last things humans may expect. The range of imagination supplies others, such as the end of the world. End-time thinking portrays contradictory conceptualizations of the end of human time. So too, spatial issues from garbage to utopia suggest contradictory ideas governing the ways we can think about them. These domains are liable to generate ambivalence unless they are absorbed into synthesizing frameworks of ideology, utopia, or other forms of transcendental thinking. The next chapter looks at the self as a collective entity, the nearest an empirically based sociological perspective can get to transcendence.

# Chapter 4

☐

# The Collective Self: I or We

Humans are not only sentient animals, but also gregarious. They spend virtually all of their waking, and much of their sleeping, lives in the presence of other human animals. As social thinkers like to point out, even when the human is alone, that animal carries a social world around in mind and heart. Sociality impregnates individuals' experience, decisions, and actions. We are in society, and in some real sense, society is in us (Berger 1963). Analysts have tried to grasp the flow and structure of the inner social reality that makes us human. Clearly, it derives from membership in collective realities. Membership in collectivities bestows a sense of a collective self: I can say "we" and know myself as more than a mere individual or bounded organism (cf. Spiegelberg 1974).

The collective self has been discussed under many rubrics: individual reductionism, social emergence, methodological individualism, dualism, social determinism, and so on. These issues revolve around a central question: what is it about our personal experience that is socially derived and best interpreted as the result of social forces? A working answer is simple: part of experience is self-generated and part is socially produced. The proper understanding of the mix is a situational and empirical question to be calculated and interpreted anew for each historical context. And the range of collective selves, as it were, goes from smaller, face-to-face groups like the family to the largest symbol-producing entities such as tribe, city, nation, race, or perhaps humankind. The present task is to search for potential ambivalence-inducing structures across selected collective selves.


## The Familial Self: How Old, Which Gender, Whose Good?

The family is, for many of us, the first and most frequented group bestowing a collective self. The family we belong to typically changes from that into which we are born to that in which we give birth, and finally, with lengthening life expectancy, to that in which we grow old and, if fortunate, die. A legacy of the psychoanalytic movement is the realization that much of self is formed within the "little world" of family life and its dramas of interpersonal relationships.

Family is the first arena of serious and self-forming conversation, the matrix of identity. As such, it is a powerful stage for the realization of self. The family is an objective, observable group of interacting individuals whose behavior and utterances could be recorded by a computer-video hook-up. It is, after all, a group of animals going about necessary activities in and around the den: eating, sleeping, waking, coupling, fighting, nurturing, disciplining, aging, and dying. A behavioral scientist could observe and record these activities better than the family members themselves. This is the family. It is a family in the same sense as a gorilla family.

As R. D. Laing (1972) emphasized, however, the human family is not quite so simple a biological or behavioral reality. That objective observable family is not the whole story. Each member has a phenomenological version of that family in his or her symbolically transformed world of thoughts, emotions, desires, and feelings. In a word, each member lives in a 'family' that is real in his or her experience and intentionality. This experiential 'family' governs our psychological lives and constitutes the phenomenological part of the entire social fact that is the family in which we live. The behavioralized family observed by the objective observer is the same for all: there is but one behavioral flow of interaction in time and space that can be observed by outsiders and enacted by the animals in the family. The experiential 'family,' however, is of necessity multiple: each member has a unique personal set of experiences that makes up his or her 'family.' The total family is an intricate overlay of each member's 'family' that exists internally and can be glimpsed only in part by other members or outsiders. Others, no matter how scientific, can only try to share person's interpretive frameworks for making sense out of the observable family. The total family is a complicated pattern of the behaviorial family and each member's 'family' woven through their shared lives.

Family patterns have structures that reduce the bewildering array somewhat. Indeed, the structures are part of the paradox that is the family. Consider that two of the deepest and most widespread social characteristics that divide humans into groups with different interests are age and gender. Age and gender are universally ascribed stratification criteria. Age is a continuous reality, yet societies appear to periodize it into stages of life. Passage from one "age," in the sense of a recognizable stage with sanctioned rights and duties, varies among societies in terms of the clarity of criteria and the formality of ritualized exits and entrances. In general, the ages through which a person typically passes reflect institutional arrangements of that society in relation to the underlying biological lifecourse of individual organisms. We all pass from dependent youth to mature adulthood and eventually back to dependent old age.

The second universal criterion for stratifying people is sex, typically conceptualized as two discrete categories of gender identity, with an occasional third or fourth such as eunuchs or androgynes. There are competing interpretations of the significance of gender stratification; is it a sociobiological fact, social convention, or divine command? Regardless of the explanation, however, studies from micro interaction to macro comparative analyses show that gender identity is a pervasive factor in the organization and stratification of society and that patriarchy is widespread. The potential explosiveness of systematic dominance of one category of humans over another is dampened by ideologies supporting age and gender privilege. Yet youth continually replace the aged in the endless battle of generations, and men and women continually vie for status and fulfillment, especially during periods of change such as the present.

As social forms, age and gender are opposites that are empirically grouped in the universal and intimate institution of the family. Extending the formal differences, we would expect that persons with opposing status-identities would experience ambiguity and ambivalence in their dealings with each other. The ambiguity and ambivalence results from their uncertainty concerning someone who is so different from self. In a sense, males and females, old and young live in different worlds with specific languages, life experiences, and societal imperatives. The greater the social difference between self and other, the less self-knowledge and self-experience help in understanding others. Yet, society takes these opposites and makes them the building blocks of that most intimate group to which many of us will ever belong.

As opposites, self would not empathically know the decisions others would be expected to make. Responses would depend on role and status inferences. This interactional ambiguity would generate confused affective responses as well, leaving the individual entirely dependent on feeling rules and normative expectations for interpreting experience. The other, and in the family, an intimate other, is both like and not like self. Clinicians note the effects of ambiguity and ambivalence within family relationships, and the likelihood that intense conflict may emerge. As a result of opposing interests linked to different status-identities, we expect that persons in different gender and age categories would experience constant conflict. Uncertain expectations and felt ambivalence appear to be related to increased levels of conflictual feelings and violent behavior. In the context of an intimate group, there is increased likelihood that such violence will be frequent and especially intense.

The componential opposites of age and gender are not the only sources of ambivalence in the family. Crosscutting age and gender is the fundamental conflict for the collective self; namely, my individual gain and the group's good. This conflict is symptomatic of the subjective reality of the family as an emergent force greater than the individuals who make it up. It is the total family comprised of each member's 'family.' It is a trans-individual force, and for that reason, difficult for individualistic moderns to understand and appreciate. The total family is not an Elysian field of saccharine togetherness and supportive warmth. Hardly! It is a trans-individual force that binds individuals together in intimate bonds of potential intensity. The intensity is the thing; the substance is our 'family'; but the situational outcome may be love or hate, caress or blow, life or death. Love grows within families—hate grows as well; at times physical violence and abuse strike (Straus, et al. 1980).

The extra-marital affair brings a third party into the husband-wife pair. Ambivalence lurks both inside and outside the pair. If the "other woman" lacks a strong self, she is ambivalent about getting involved with a married man, especially if faced with the dilemmas of permanence or a break-up and additional affairs (Richardson 1985). From the side of assumed marital fidelity, when the wronged spouse discovers the affair, he or she is pulled in two directions: to leave because of pain from a negated past; or to stay because of the scariness of an uncertain future (Vaughan 1989). Whatever ambivalence the married pair felt previously, an affair compounds an exclusive marriage by contradicting previous definitions of their shared past, present, and future.

Family intensity flows from the objective features of nearness, frequency of interaction, overlapping time and space, shared resources, and closely knit fate. These objective features are symbolically transformed into the inner life of members and underwrites each person's 'family.' The 'family' legitimates sacrifice as well as exploitation; it justifies executioners as well as victims. Quite simply, family is often the first moral battleground on which the

ambivalent dilemmas of modern life are joined. The issue
that appears to lie within today's struggle is the tension
between my personal gain and the commonweal of the
group. In a word, the struggle that I and We wage within my
experience concerns whose good is on top, Mine or Ours?
Am I to build a Me or an Us?

### *The Institutional Self: Service and Loyalty or Profit and Opportunism?*

In a widely read article, Ralph Turner (1976) finds a
modern dilemma in the tension between individual impulse
and institutional commitment. It is an issue that has
engaged social thinkers since Socrates freely took his life in
fulfillment of a law and trial that he judged wrong-headed.
The issue is the proper relationship between the individual
and the collective self, or more specifically between the
individual and the institution. I will touch on institutional
sectors with an eye for their contradictory demands. For
example, the idealism of those far-away days of the 1960s
was captured in the then stirring phrase, "Ask not what
your Country can do for you, but what you can do for your
Country." In the merest twitch of historical time, the 1980s
re-legitimated the contradictory query, "What's in it for
me?" These tensions find expression in the institutional sectors that make up the typical sequence of status doors the
individual must open and walk through.

In the educational sector, teachers and pupils are
stretched between the goals of reproducing status by training for jobs versus developing individuals for critical thinking, but not too critical. The battle goes under a number of
shibboleths such as liberal education versus relevant education; critical thinking versus education for citizenship;
handing on Western "Civilization" versus learning the
human story; or finding the best talent whatever the cost
versus reproducing parents' privilege and wealth. Are
teachers trainers, hired hands, and civil servants, or are
they professors of the best efforts to understand self, soci-

ety, and nature? Do they respond to market demand, or do they teach what they believe important, regardless of students' or society's demands? These questions catch some of the contradictory expectations in the role of teacher or professor. The latter title makes the fundamental dilemma more transparent: just what is a person in the almost sacred position of educating youth "professing"? And is what the teacher professes the same as what parents, government, and critics believe will educate or lead youth from their unformed and uninformed state into that condition of knowledge and attitudes that powerful gatekeepers deem appropriate? Who belongs to "The Dead Poets' Society"?

Dual pressures are firmly felt in colleges and universities. Pressures are particularly acute in a Nation in which expectations are for everyone to have the chance to go to college, and in which upward mobility or better chances are tied to a college degree. In the Carnegie Foundation's report, *College,* Ernest Boyer reports conflict between individuality and community at the heart of undergraduate reality (66). Furthermore, he senses tension between utilitarian careerism and knowledge for life crackling throughout all ranks of the colleges.

These tensions bring ambivalence to Boyer's pen in crucial contexts, although he does not use it in a methodical way. He refers to its presence among students, faculty, and administrators. From a national survey, Boyer (1987) reports that students are ambivalent about the pressure for careerist courses and the desire for general education (85); indeed, about one-third of the students would quit college if there were not a strong tie-in with the job market (102); faculty as a collective body reflects ambivalence in that about one-half prefer teaching their "limited specialities" and students with a "clear idea" of career, yet about one-half say that undergraduate education would be improved with more general courses (107); administrators are ambivalently anxious about their responsibility for students' lives outside the classroom as colleges have switched from parent to clinician in the last thirty years (179, 203).

In general, students are ambivalent to the teaching-learning nexus as the chase for grades corrodes the search for insight. Boyer refers to ambivalence in religious attitudes among students: three fourths believe in a judging God, but far fewer think that most students are religious or that they themselves are more religious now that they are in college (188). It is as though they want to believe in something even as they pursue specialized, job-oriented knowledge that threatens or is indifferent to such belief.

Contradictory educational expectations can be caught in a phrase like "critically informative." Either of these characteristics without the other leaves teaching or learning maimed, and the transmission and interpretation of knowledge inadequate. The conjoint act of professing and learning, the creative confrontation between the conventional wisdom of the group and the ever reborn grasp of that wisdom by the next generation, must combine the best of transmission and criticism. No rote learning of classics, recitation of formulae from one tradition, or eclectic mix from East and West can prepare intellect and emotion to handle modern ambiguity and ambivalence. In the absence of a universally accepted framework to reconcile opposites of cognition and affect, the modern must learn to live with the tension and turn it into creative motivation. Can educators recognize and resolve ambivalence and so motivate others?

Motivation generates human labor that embodies it. The occupational structure, however, provides an interesting tension of its own. There is the tension between alienating repetitive drudgery that critics of industrial and international capitalism argue characterizes the mills, sweatshops, and conveyer-belt factories of the modern world, and the creative work of some utopian imagination or of skilled craftsmen and independent shopkeepers during earlier periods of Western history. The fundamental tension is between the drudgery that large-scale production demands, and creative or shared responsibility that workers find satisfying. The quest for a balance goes on, with models from Japan suggesting that traditional order and shopfloor discipline can combine to raise productivity or some drudgery can be handed over to robotic hands. What effect different controls over the workplace have on workers from other cultures awaits further study. It is not likely that the fundamental tension can be resolved permanently.

Richard Sennet and Jonathon Cobb (1973) discern a subtle kind of ambivalence in their working class respondents. Workers both recognize the legitimacy of their managers and owners to judge them and resent superiors' right and knowledge to do so. Workers are both angry and ambivalent about their anger (79). There is ambivalence in the discrepant identity of a shop foreman who must demote a friend. The tension of friendship and authority is too strong: ambivalence is resolved by the death of the friendship (204).

Stories of downward mobility from the middle class present us with persons who are both committed to core American values and stigmatized by self and other for failure to realize those very values. As Katherine Newman puts it, an over-forty unemployed man who claims to be a "talented ex-manager is a living contradiction" (1989: 92). She finds similar contradictions among those falling down the ladder of success as they struggle over whether to borrow money from family members, move to a poorer neighborhood, remarry, or tell the truth to their children who believe the Horatio Alger story even as their father-absent family sinks to make ends meet.

Characteristics of business institutions lead to ambivalence. The employee is asked to be loyal to companies that have no local identity, indeed, in increasing cases, no national identity. Work may, without warning, be moved to another part of the country or world. On the other hand, a "foreign" company may move into the neighborhood with different work traditions and employer-employee relationships. Employees may feel a sense of loyalty to the company, but with a stronger sense of looking out for self. International business increases the split between laborer and self as well as between labor and management when it overlays their differing interests with national differences.

At the top of the occupational ladder, we find professionals moving toward more formally organized and bureaucratized structures. Neighborhood doctors join the clinic, hospital, medical center, health maintenance organization, or group practice and become professionals who are also 9 to 5 bureaucrats. Scientists work for large institutes on regular work schedules. Academics win grants from governmental agencies or large businesses, patent their discoveries, and start their own business undertakings while keeping privileged professorial status. As academicians, they are protected by professorial prestige and security while they compete in the marketplace with other venturing entrepreneurs.

The position of the salaried or bureaucratized professional combines two contradictory codes into a single status. Salaried individuals work for someone else and follow others' priorities. Bureaucrats follow standardized rules with predictable patterns of decision making and action. Professionals, on the other hand, are autonomous actors pursuing truth and practice in accord with their critical judgment and expert knowledge. A client may wonder whether the business person-medical professional is maximizing profit or the client's well being. The split structure of the business-professional status elicits ambivalent responses.

Within academe, pressure from standardized national norms of productivity and "mainstream" research and writing pushes professors to profess their aspirations for upward mobility. In the struggle, they shelve ideas for writing novels or critical essays unacceptable to the mainline journals that function as gatekeepers to disciplinary prestige. Creative intellectual inquiry is dampened to conformity to the reward structures of tenure and purse.

The upshot of this glimpse at occupations is that there are pressures pushing and pulling in opposite directions. Where the pressures are particularly severe, we would expect responses such as burnout, distancing from work, alienation from employers, and other pathologies of work. Only systematic empirical study can tell us if ambivalence works this way and if its effect is on the increase. Special insight is likely to come from studies of ex-officials about-to-be lobbyists and high flying financiers with illegal information as two of the most profitable and characteristic occupations of the modern scene.

## Working at Leisure

When not in school or at work, Americans are probably at play, actively or passively. The divide between work and play is hardly clear, but leisure is what we do with time at our disposal. Leisure lies outside the claims of the institutions that surround us and the demands of those who people our personal relationships. A main function of leisure time is the denial or affirmation of the way of life that dominates non-leisure time.

For the moment, reverse the usual viewpoint and place yourselves in the world of leisure time taken as the paramount real world, and view the institutions of the workaday world as getting meaning from leisure. This reverses the usual phenomenological view in which the workaday world is the "paramount reality" into which our lives are "geared" whether we like it or not (see Schutz 1962). Although, in general, Schutz is correct to give paramount reality to the necessities derived from the workaday world, we wish to take the opposite view to get a perspective on leisure.

What are the relationships between the leisure world and non-leisure reality? There are three broad possibilities: reenforcement, contradiction, or irrelevance. Leisure that re-enforces workaday identities is exemplified by employee social clubs, athletic leagues, religious recreational groups, or ethnic and neighborhood leisure centers. The principle of organization and criterion of membership follow from identities that individuals have in the workaday and typically serious world. These extensions of the real world help members to continue performing adequately and perhaps enhance their ability to move up a social rung or two. Such were the clubs, fraternities, and brotherhoods that helped successive ethnic groups enter the class system of the United States, and the use of male titles portrays the traditional link between the non-domestic workaday world and male gender. Reenforcement of the values and institutions of the workaday world was channeled through the leisure of males since they moved between the two worlds in sufficiently permanent numbers. Leisure-time links strengthened members to go back to daily work and meet their obligations of family, job, God, and Country.

Contradictions between leisure time pursuits and the workaday world appear on two dimensions. There are the reforming, or in a few cases revolutionary groups. The former are dominated by the historical struggle of the labor unions, while anarchist or revolutionary types have not been as salient in this Nation's history. Reformist groups appear across the ideological spectrum from the political left to the right, and from ethical societies to civil rights or anti-nuclear associations. Unions arose in opposition to business and ownership power and evolved into social support structures for workers, and in some cases, into partnerships between owners and laborers. International and technological pressures are pushing unions into weaker positions as transnational capitalism gains mobility and strength. Furthermore, helping agencies take over social support functions as working class and ethnic associations weaken.

Within the cultural domain there is a choice of reenforcing or contradictory forms of leisure. One can see *Rambo* or *Rocky* and cheer, or *Platoon* and cry. There are drug cultures and protest clothing available for those opposed to the central values paraded in the workaday world. There are also chic drug scenes to be made with the successful and about-to-be successful gentry. There are the hidden-away bohemian groves, watering holes, and power dens where the upwardly well placed rub shoulders at country clubs, squash clubs, and racing clubs. Devotees of these clubs outnumber the revolutionary cells of experimenting students or unarmed intellectuals who reenforce only each other's theoretical mistakes in predicting the short-term downfall of financial capitalism's computer links from London, New York, and Tokyo (awaiting Moscow and Beijing).

Finally, there are leisure time pursuits that are thought by some participants to be irrelevant to the dilemmas of the day. Social scientists would not stop with participants' own accounts of leisure's relevance to the workaday world. The unintended consequences of participants' activities can be seen as reenforcing or contradicting that real world. There are likely to be causal links, no matter how tenuous and difficult to see, tying what we do to the survival of the kind of society in which we live. Watching vacuous TV sitcoms may seem irrelevant, but it could be a prime move as the world turns modern.

### Neighborhoods: Open or Closed?

Most of us live in neighborhoods. With neighbors, we juggle the openings provided by nearness to form working relationships while keeping the distance required for our own lifestyles. We no doubt carry in our minds and hearts some nostalgia for that romanticized version of village life in traditionalists' talk and novelists' visions. The neighborhood works as a miniature of the vast cosmos.

The imperative of American atomism, on the other hand, is that each person-group, whether family or not, is entitled to its own lifestyle, as long as it stays within the law and the tolerance levels of neighbors. The public order of municipalities and suburbs balances on a seesaw with the law at one end and local propriety at the other, that is, neighbors acceptance or rejection. Municipal codes and higher-order laws are more or less detailed, with libertarians wanting less and law and order conservatives or communitarians wanting more, but there is never enough detail to cover all eventualities and the ingenuity of the human animal who lives next door.

What balances differences between law and the *sensus communis* of the neighborhood? It is that invisible but real line neighbors have drawn about what is acceptable when everything is taken into account. That line is drawn with the neighborhood equalizer: the complaint. A community code states that non-domestic animals may not be kept in the yard. Yet, a "wild" rabbit in an outside cage is a favorite of neighborhood children and allowed to live a most suburban existence. No horses ought to be kept unless the lot is five acres or more. Yet, the remnant farmhouse keeps a horse cum companions in the yard, but no neighbor complains because of a larger principle of fair play toward those who lived here before the tract developers moved in the backhoes. Tolerance is essential for healthy neighboring with the right mix of daily togetherness and social distance.

Intimacy breeds strong emotions. The duality of family as the hearth of love and the pit of violence is documented. It takes strong social bonds and an overriding legitimacy to keep persons intimate through it all. Neighbors have neither the strength of bonds nor the legitimacy of familism based on affinity, blood, sex, and common legal and economic fate. Literature bares witness to the straits of neighbors who get too close, have a falling out, and become unspeaking enemies who must still share the same view, fence, alley, wall, or corridor.

The principle of a neighborhood village is reenforced by allowing only others like us to live by us. Residential segregation, for example, is the skeleton of racial segragation in the United States. In an open society, residentiality is putatively available to anyone who can pay for it in the real estate market. The official American way is segregation by money or class, not by race or religion. The empirical American way, however, is by all four criteria governing who lives next to whom.

A dilemma is posed: do we want open neighborhoods restricted only by the amount of the down payment and ability to meet the monthly mortgage; or do we want the neighborhood village peopled by persons like us? If we opt for the former, what is to keep out someone whom I do not wish to accept as a neighbor and whose son I do not want to meet my daughter, like the scion from an organized crime family? Or, what is to stop a religious cult or Hell's Angels cadre from moving in if the zoning laws are not tight enough? On the other hand, who wants to live in a village with all the small town controls, social idiocy, as Marx may argue, and ethnic purity that smallness implies? Is Rosedale an urban village that should remain white?

The dilemma is discernible in the nitty gritty of neighbors' existence. Outlandish paint on the house; rusting cars in the yard; smells of strange food; uncontrolled children; periodic pilfering; backbiting gossip—all combine into massively real facts that make up the neighborhood the way bricks make up the graveyard wall. Nor is it merely a question of conflicting ways of life, as real as that is. Differences in living styles relate to the ranking of privileged symbols and judgments of what is aesthetically in line with the class structure. In other words, getting the wrong neighbors translates into falling property values, and homes are the largest dollar and emotional investment of many people.

Neighborhoods enter the emotional world of family continuity as parents watch for youths' romantic ties likely to follow lines of nearness and frequency of contact. Endogamy and the mating game are related to neighborhood in ways that add great concern for parents, especially for the economically and racially minded. The history and financing of public education links the quality of schooling directly to the political, social, and economic power of the neighborhood. And, as every parent knows, education is the mechanism for upward mobility as well as mate selection. Finally, there are patterns of deviance and conformity, especially in the realm of drugs, drink, and crime, that are feared in the neighborhoods.

Neighbors do not want any "element" that may shift the delicate balance, if they are pleased; or they may want to get rid of some, if the neighborhood has, as we say, gone down hill. To live up on Beacon Hill or Telegraph Hill is also to be on the right side of the tracks, or more recently, right side of the highway, to use another metaphor for the way neighborhoods are physically and symbolically divided. So ambivalence between open and closed neighborhoods goes on as we wrestle with the model of village or suburb in our evaluations of where we live.

In other historical eras, a neighborhood was the extent

of one's social being. The modern world, however, has seen the incorporation of virtually the entire earth into a system of nation-states. With few exceptions, the five billion plus of the earth's dwellers are governed by a state apparatus. In recent years, also, the centralization and growth of power at the center of the state characterizes totalitarian, socialist, and democratic societies. Historical forces have broadened the inclusion of peoples under the rule and care of the centralized state. The states in the United States are governed by Washington, D.C., and the tribes and ethnic regions of the Third World are incorporated into or destroyed by the all-inclusive state.

### *Centri—Petal or Fugal?*

Depending on one's political vision for advanced societies, the centralized state is cause for joy, depression, or both. Some trust the state to be built up at the center, others distrustingly want it dismantled and spread around. At the birth of America, Barry Schwartz (1987) finds deep-seated ambivalence toward the founding figure, George Washington himself. America won its freedom by defeating a king; it was not to create another in his place. Yet, in the elitism of colonial society, Washington was the object of awe and gratitude. As the most powerful man, George Washington was an object of both esteem and suspicion, admiration and fear. Schwartz notes that "Ambivalence . . . made American hero worship distinctive" (39). This ambivalence evokes that which anthropologists report finding in members of Pacific societies toward their leaders or "Big Men" who must balance solidarity and strength in a "dilemma of dominance" (White and Kirkpatrick, 1985: 338–346). Others find that ambivalence within and toward the nation-state is a feature of modern civil religion (cf. Wuthnow 1988a).

The paradox of trust-distrust toward centralized governments continues. Given the increasing interdependence of international interests and the growing power of the military, the trust-distrust at the international level underwrites a powerful state apparatus. In the social economy, the state enters as arbiter of last resort for the survival benefits of its members. It takes on the distribution of goods and services necessary for the good life society claims to offer. An emerging Third World society may distribute literacy; an advanced society may hand out retirement security or a modicum of food and housing; and a post-modern society may make the freedom of elite members its primary goal. Whatever substantive differences there are among societies, their resemblance is in the central power of the bureaucratized state in contact with individuals who simultaneously trust and distrust its offices. Paying taxes highlights the split for those who approve state power in defense but not in welfare, or for others who think the opposite. The state is a two-headed creation.

Peter Berger has argued that voluntary "mediating structures" have been weakened in modern societies. As a result, individuals must deal directly with the state or its bureaucratic agencies. The modern institutional self is defined in terms of bureaucracy. Nor is it just the state that is bureaucratic. With transnational corporations on a par with some nations in size and power, their structures are just as powerfully bureaucratic, though they are classier and better appointed. Analysts of religion, as we see in the next chapter, note that modern religious organizations are likewise characterized by the power of their bureaucracies. If the content, as it were, of the dominant relationship in advanced societies is that of the individual and the state, then the form of that relationship is the client identity of the individual linked to a bureaucratic other, analogous to the poetic existence of "pedro ortega."

Dilemmas and contradictions are associated with bureaucratization, even in the best of contexts. In the worst, contradictions become perplexing: take someone who has rushed into an emergency room needing immediate attention only to be accosted with questions of insurance coverage and admission forms. In some cases, the bureaucratic anteroom becomes the proscenium for life and death dramas, as injured bodies are refused entry and sent across town because bodies have the wrong bureaucratic identity of address, insurance card, or even race. The client's attitude toward the standardized expertise of the bureaucrat may well be an ambivalently mistrusting dependence. Such ambivalence has been discovered at the heart of the healing relationship, perhaps the exemplary client-bureaucrat case: the link between patient and doctor (cf. Barber 1983).

In their attitudes toward the state, individuals seem torn between the free self of the classical American myth and the entitled self confronting today's exigencies. To put the dilemma in simple terms, Americans are split over their deep sense of duty and autonomy and an emerging eagerness for entitlement and welfare. The former values are associated with a judgment that the state ought to play a minimal part in the domestic life of society. Individuals performing their duty do the rest. Civic republicanism is, after all, a founding virtue of this free democratic society (cf. Bellah et al. 1985).

On the other side of dutiful citizenship, the state places individual autonomy at the heart of its priorities. Nothing should interfer with individual freedom. The state's principle domestic function is to stand as a silent partner behind citizens' contracts freely entered. The actions of dutiful citizens and the protection of individual freedoms undergird a democratic society. The remaining task is to extend these democratic freedoms to more and more of the world. These principles seem so obvious to Americans as to become an unquestioned ideology worth dying for, and in the hands of "Irangate" back-office types, lying for, even to fellow citizens and the officials, paradoxically.

On the other hand, there is a growing sense that the state should guarantee reasonable development of everyone's potential. There is an increasing demand for entitlement. Some think of it as turning the accepted order upside down (cf. Yankelovich 1982). Imagine autonomous citizens in a free democratic society demanding that the state provide adequate housing, food, medical care, old age pensions, and even a college education. Rather than duty, the issue is entitlement; rather than autonomy, the demand is sharing and enlarging the commonweal. The argument concerns the priorities of a democratic society that has, for the time being at least, sufficient resources. Does not democracy require the relevant participation of its citizenry? Then does it not require adequately educated, healthy, secure citizens with sufficient dignity to underwrite democratic participation?

The older shibboleth, "I worked for everything I got!" is being replaced with, "I've got a right to everything I need to work!" Is not the moral worth of a society judged by the way it treats its weaker members: the young, the old, and the sick? Should not democracies, then, lead the way in this moral dimension of modern affluent societies? The debate between entitlement and autonomy goes on, and the structural implications of each struggle against the other. The simple language of games and war in which all compete against all for one prize creates only one winner but many losers. The sense of fair play and justice that underlay American society does not look unambiguously on the King Rat scene in which one operator cleans out the rest. On the other hand, do we not admire the King of the Mountain?

Institutionalized relationships with the environment show a split analogous to that of duty versus entitlement, or profit versus commonweal. In a broad-brush picture, the institutional self has moved from a kind of subsistence relationship with the physical environment to one of productive manipulation and continuous consumption. Social ideologies are formulated to justify and legitimate such relationships. Ideology provides the basis for a mythically transformed life that is thought to be in accord both with the laws of nature and the laws of God. Humans hunted and thanked God; they farmed and thanked God; they manufactured and thanked God; and now they are consuming and thanking God all the same. In spite of a certain rationalization of these relationships, there seems to be something numinous in the hunting, agricultural, and in general, "natural" exploits. In the manufacturing and consuming ways of life, however, the numinous is filtered.

The link between western Christianity and capitalism

shows interesting ambivalence in the point-counterpoint of Max Weber's analysis of *The Protestant Ethic and the Spirit of Capitalism*. In brief, he argued that religious ideologies typically provide a set of motives that preserved traditional ways of life. A paradoxical result of what he called this-worldly ascetic Protestantism, however, is that it fired powerful motives in the pursuit of salvation that believers had to find in their daily lives. Worldly success became the sure sign of their election by God who predetermines everyone's salvation or dammation. What an unbelievable consolation in the face of ultimate anxiety!

Signs of salvation were limited to productive success, not to the consumption of what the saints had gained. The entrepreneurial saints' lives remained abstemious and ascetic. They sought salvation through incessant work and condemned frivolity, akin to the set-faced seriousness of America's Gothic fathers and mothers. As capitalism became the air that western Christendom breathed, the religious life gradually pealed back to reveal motives no longer fired by the stirrings of salvation. Capitalism came to rock its own cradles and to form this-worldly acquisitive consciences.

Ascetic this-worldly Protestantism, according to Weber, provided paradoxical motives that drove believers to feats of economic production but not consumption. With modernity, consumption has taken center court. The United States appears to lead the way in per capita consumption from calories eaten to dollars spent. Many consume with no need for a religious ethic of consumption analogous to the Protestant ethic of production. Hedonism is as American as eating an entire apple pie. For millions, however, there is a Protestant ethic with a twist analogous to Weber's argument concerning the spread of capitalism. Fundamentalist and Pentecostal "televangelists" argue that if you, the viewer, are right with God and ask Him for any material "blessing," then He will rain rewards upon you. Like a potlatch, these religions bless material gain and baptize believers' unlimited consumption as a new sign of God's salvific approval. In a capitalist society, we know that wealth is an essential

means to freedom and dignity. It is a small symbolic step to
see it as a sign of salvation as well.

To show that God is materially bountiful here and
now, you need only follow the lifestyle of the televangelists
themselves. The primary story concerns those televangelists who taught, not this-worldly asceticism as a sign of
salvation and an ironical motive for hard work and self-
denial, but this-worldly consumerism. God wants us to be
happy, enjoy ourselves, and have what we want on earth.
His blessings include earthly mansions and an air-condi-
tioned dog house.

So there is an ethic of consumption; but alas and ironically, it is aimed at those who are not the primary consumers in advanced capitalism. The televangelist's audience is likely to be at the edge of the mainline American
success story: older, rural, fundamentalist, and less than
wealthy. Yet, consuming, or helping their televangelists to
consume, signals salvation, and thus supplies that supreme
motive that all believers seek. Feeling saved is being saved,
and there is nothing like it in all the world. Ambivalence
toward their life situation disappears beneath the saving
cloak of Jesus. Transforming material things into signs of
salvation removes ambiguity from them, and, amazing
grace, from my life of doubt and trial as well. That most
American of religious messages, salvation through consumption, takes Weber's thesis and stands it on its head.

Those who do not accept televangelistic transformation
of consumption into salvation are left with their ambivalence. There are, to be sure, ideologies to justify consumption: needs, profits, rights, entitlements, quasi-religions, and
simply, hedonism. None of these, however, anoints with the
conviction of salvation, and each must be squared with contradictory values: sacrifice, fairness, duties, service, alternative quasi-religious views, and secular asceticism.

Consider some accounts persons give for consuming: I
earned it, so I can do what I want with it; It belongs to me, so
I have the right to use it for myself; As an American, I may
use as much as I can afford; God allowed me to have it, so
He must want me to enjoy it before He comes again; I like it

so I will do it. Against these accounts, there is another
stream of American values: it is not fair that I have so much
while others are starving through no fault of their own, like
children, the disabled, the elderly, and the sick; I have an
obligation to contribute to my Country which has given me
so much; The American way is to work with and for others;
God has given me so much so that I may help others; finally,
No matter how much I have, it is best to live simply. These
accounts vie one with another, but the trend is toward
greater consumption among those who can pay. If it is not a
sign of salvation with the consolation that brings, at least
consumption is a certain sign of materialist success: the single universal currency that Americans of whatever ideological persuasion understand and can translate into symbolic
or social goods like status, freedom, prestige, and power.

Underlying the modern institutional self is a fundamental dilemma. Moderns live in an increasingly massive society, that is, a society of high population density and great
social distance from positions of power and decision making, illustrated by hugh bureaucracies. The dilemma is this:
no single act I perform really makes any difference, so why
don't I go on making decisions only in terms of what's in it
for me? As someone said when challenged for tossing an
empty beer bottle on the side of the road, "My percentage
contribution to litter is too small for me to worry about, and
I wanted to get rid of the bottle now." Why should not everyone "get rid of the bottle now" if that serves one's interests?
Bottle riddance is a litter side of the well-analyzed free rider
problem, the dilemma that a cheating individual comes out
ahead as long as everyone else follows the rules.

What reason could there be for limiting my best interests as I define them? Is not that what the American ethos is
all about, and what individualism is? And freedom? If I want
to burn rubbish or burn electricity or gas or coal or oil or
whatever, then I may do it. If I wish to use pesticides, herbi-
cides, fungicides, insecticides, and any other "cide" on my
lawn to make it green and lush then why may I not do so? If I
as a farmer plan to use nitrate fertilizer to increase my yield,
then I shall do so.

Examples multiply themselves. Think of activities you favor and state your own case. The content changes, but the dilemma remains. What principle can persuade a person *not* to act in such a way as to maximize his or her individual gain? Why should I limit my consumption of anything as long as I want it. Do I owe self-denial to my ancestors; to my consociates; to my descendents; to future generations? Nothing that I, *as a consuming individual,* do will matter one iota in calculations determining the future of human life. I may eat, drink, consume, yes, even waste, to my stomach's content, and the earth will not be tipped off its course nor jetted into a preferable one. In a single phrase, as an individual, the consequences of my actions are literally inconsequential. No instrument measuring the course of history could be sensitive enough to record even my existence, not to mention this or that empty bottle. If my actions, qua individual, are inconsequential, then why in the world should I limit my consumption? Why should I conserve? Either way, consuming or conserving, no one can measure my impact on a global or even local scale. It is totally unreasonable to take inconsequential actions into account as determining what I should do. I will, therefore, go on consuming at whatever rate pleases me. Thus, I write the consumers' ethic.

The most ardent individualist, however, knows that the dilemma is part of the paradox of large numbers. What is reasonable for an individual is totally unreasonable for a large population. What is an inconsequential act becomes very consequential indeed, if all were to do it. If one person drops a candy wrapper on the city sidewalk, it remains a candy wrapper. If many do it, it becomes litter and an expensive urban annoyance. One bug in the house is bemusing, but a horde of bugs is a menace. The issue is the litterbug paradox. There is no litter without many violators, yet each violator is an inconsequential bug acting for self-interest. The same may be said for virtually every social aspect of modern life. That is what it means to be an individual in a mass.

In an individualistic culture, the dilemma is severe. How can an individual form a conscience that motivates him or her to act as though the self were primarily a member of a collective, and not to act for the individual interests of self? This query scores the abstract unreality of individualism. In brute fact and easily traced empirical links if we take the entire situation into account, the individual never acts solely as individual, unless he or she were in a sealed capsule outside empirical systems causally related to those of other earthlings. As far as we know, there is no such capsule within any possible readership, and perhaps not in our cosmos. Not groups, but individual monads, are the abstractions of fevered minds.

Individualism is a mistaken abstraction translated into feelings and motivations via the fallacy of misplaced concreteness: we naturally take a mental category, e.g., individual, and assume that there are actual empirical instances existing just as we define the category. If we define an individual as a being who exists in, by, and of self, we naturally believe that there are such, when in social fact, there are not. Furthermore, the category of individual can be symbolically transformed into an idealized cultural value and become not only a mental mistake but a motivational ideal informing ethics, laws, and decisions. Finally, this fallacious understanding can be internalized as the most *real* aspect of self and the focus of feelings that give it a sense of reality beyond other personal experience. My sense of self as an individual becomes the core of personal identity.

## *We and/or I?*

If this were the whole story, individuality would add nothing to the theme of ambivalence. Ideology often overrides empirically based perceptions, and eventually we, as ideologues, make up an idealized world we mistake for the real world. The empirical world, however, forces itself upon us at critical junctures. The litter blowing around city streets strikes our eyes; excess nitrates in the soil enter our water and public awareness, if there are empirically based avenues of knowledge to monitor the flow; spruce needles turn brown and fall at our feet from acid rain; vacationers get overheated psyches in traffic jams blocking interstate highways; and, in general, the paradox of the law of large numbers is repeated for anyone living in, around, or downwind from major population centers. There are, in other words, sources for a sense of ourselves as part of something larger than an individual. It may be a negative sense of common fate grounded in the inexorable natural processes begun or heated up by the paradoxical accumulation of "purely" individual actions.

Hence, we feel ambivalence. We wish to go on acting as though we were nothing but individuals. Nevertheless, we know that even if we truly were nothing but individuals, the cumulative effect of millions of individuals acting, so each thinks, independently, means that no one's fate is empirically independent of others. As members of an aggregate like one pebble on a beach, if that is the strongest sense of collective self that individualists can muster, each must consider his or her fate as though self were an aggregate actor having a cumulative effect on persons, things, and social relationships.

Even individuals who are ordinary property offenders, that is, non-professionals who commit crimes against property, experience ambivalence (Frazier and Meisenhelder 1985). Feelings both motivated and followed from the crime. The consequent feelings appear to be compound emotions based on serial perceptions of what they as individuals did and how others responded to the deed. Eventually, these self-defined and publically labeled "criminals" felt both individual satisfaction and personal guilt or shame.

Each person is divided at the heart of his or her motivation, feelings, and decisions. Do I act in terms of my so-believed individual interests? Or do I act in terms of the aggregate outcome of millions of individuals, each believing that his or her action is independent and trivial in its consequences? The aggregate outcome of self-seeking can be tragic. As the holiday cruise ship enters the harbor, hundreds of individuals make what each takes to be an individual decision to run to the other side of the deck for a view of the Statue of Liberty. Each portside run is trivial, but the run of all is tragic as the boat lists sharply and capsizes. The slightly queasy probability that humans may now be running to the port side of the ship gives us second thoughts, and, if dwelt upon, generates ambivalence.

There is a second type of identity that suggests ambivalence of this sort. It concerns a person who has both ideologies, individualism and collectivism. These ideologies link the person to different reference groups: e.g., libertarians and socialists; or more likely, the family and the market place of individual mobility; or loyalty to traditional values of a minority group and a burning desire to succeed on one's own wit; or struggling to make the collectivist currents of the Judeo-Christian tradition relevant to the self-centered modernist scene. Such persons would feel ambivalence because their self is split into two ideological or identity commitments, not because of the paradoxical law of large numbers, the litterbug paradox, or the portside run.

A plausible theme in American history is the ambivalence that immigrant peoples experienced and resolved by embracing the "American Way of Life." A study of East European peasant-immigrants around the turn of the century point out the ambivalence they felt (Morawska 1987). They were deeply torn between identities and commitments to the old country, their local ethnic community, and their traditional way of life on the one hand, and their desire to identify with America, the larger social context, and new ways of ownership, thinking, and feeling on the other. Perhaps as many as one third resolved the mixed feelings by returning home. The two thirds who remained embraced the American solution. Perhaps, too, as I suspect, the pain of ambivalence motivated a tight embrace that stifled cries on behalf of the old way of life.

A final aspect of an institutional self concerns images of the United States on the international scene. Recent decades offer contradictory images. There is the Fortress of Democracy that entered the international stage as the major protagonist during and after World War II. The following years were a *pax Americana* as military, financial, economic, and social hegemony emanated from both shores of the U.S.A. The Marshall Plan for rebuilding Europe became the great symbol. It was followed by the disquieting sounds of the so-called Korean War that halted in an unsettling draw. In the historical time of a split second, the Vietnam struggle engaged the Country in gradual, ambiguous, and eventually, totally ambivalent directions in yet another undeclared "war." From the Fortress of Democracy, the U.S.A. became "Amerika" and a wedge was driven into the national identity of many Americans. For the first time, many could not simply assert, "My Country, right or wrong," or assume that their Country was fighting a crusade for freedom, democracy, and God. The empirical situation outstripped any single definition of national purpose. Only ideologues had answers that stifled doubt in foreign policy.

Ambivalence toward the Vietnam War is aesthetically captured in the definition, selection, and additions surrounding the Memorial to that social contradiction, an "undeclared war." The contradictions generate a "genre problem" (Wagner-Pacifici and Schwartz,1987): how can we commemorate the undeclared war without deciding the moral worth of losing that "war" and at the same time honoring those who fought and died in it? The answer is not clear; there is apparently no accepted semiotic for memorializing defeat, since monuments are re-affirmations of a nation's identity, ideals, triumphs, or superficially, a civil religious moral unity. What is to be done if there is no morally unified definition but there is a felt need to memorialize the sacrifice of thousands of obedient victims? One answer is played out in the ongoing construction of the Vietnam Veterans Memorial: a humble, somber, sacred listing of the dead below ground level; a later addition of upright, courageous, but sadly victimized soldiers; and a flag whose inscription recognizes the "war" as "difficult circumstances" and symbolizes personal sacrifice and national ideals amidst moral doubt and confused defeat. In short, the function of the Memorial is not to proclaim a moral unity that does not exist, but to reveal a deeper moral truth: a nation struggling with contradictions in its collective memory and ambivalence toward one watershed event in that memory.

American attitudes toward the Soviet Union in recent years indicate ambivalence on the international scene. It seems that Americans both fear the Russians and want to work with them, both accept and reject them (see Yankelovich and Doble 1984). The dilemma is clearly symbolized by the words and actions of a President of the United States. Ronald Reagan, for example, calls the Russians an "evil empire" that does only bad and must be opposed at every turn. On the other hand, it is good to meet with the Russians to work toward a nuclear arms deal.

The American international stance is an unpredictable combination of pragmatism and ideology. This combination appears in the attitudes of the citizenry as well. Survey respondents with presumably strong ideological viewpoints, such as those who hold fundamentalist religious beliefs, have more extreme views about the Soviet Union. An instance is the identification of Russia with Gog and Magog in the Old Testament in the thinking of some dispensationalist fundamentalist writers (Lindsey 1977; van Impe 1984). It is likely that such an ideology provides certain definitions of events and overcomes ambivalence. It remains to be seen how massive realignments in international relations and the Soviet sphere affects Americans' feelings toward former enemies or wayward client states.

## Summary

Although ambivalence lives within individual experience, the person is always more than a mere individual. This chapter touches on collective aspects of the self, even within a culture based on individuality. Individualism as such is ideological and non-empirical: it is simply not true that any person or act is merely an individual event as such. One goal of this chapter is to stamp the empirical priority of the social self in our thinking, and maybe make us a bit more ambivalent!

The first collective reality most of us incorporate into our experience is the family into which we are born. Something of this collective self persists through the rest of our lives as we live through our original family and probably go on to make up another generation of families of procreation. Here we learn firsthand about the dilemma between What's in it for me? and What ought I do for us? This dualism sets the stage for ambivalence through other aspects of our collective selves.

A brief review of dilemmas that face us if we think of our selves in the context of education, work, leisure, neighborhood, the state, and religion suggests that there are structures of ambivalence at each of these empirical turns. In fact, individuals exist as collective selves, and at times we must experience our selves as parts of collectivities. Collectivities are institutionalized; they confront us as organized networks of persons working with rules and goals that define how they will deal with us and the world. We, in turn, learn how to deal with institutions, and in so doing, internalize that way of acting whether the ideology of individualism allows us to admit it or not. We experience ourselves as individuals and as collective selves. This is reason enough for feeling ambivalent.

Two pervasive aspects of collective existence that generate ambivalence are: the paradox of large numbers, i.e., my single act is trivial, but if many do the same, the outcome is powerful; and belief in an ethic of consumption in the face of evidence that increasing consumption fuels threats to the life-supporting environment. A revealing application of these reflections is to those brands of fundamentalist religion that offer an ethic of consumption and self-indulgence: a reversal of the Weberian thesis that ascetic Protestantism helped give birth to capitalism through hard work and self-denial. The next chapter tries to show how some moderns are inclined to accept a religious answer to a powerful source of ambivalence.

# Chapter 5

◻

# Joyful Disaster: Religion as Certain Ambivalence

Inherited wisdom recognizes the impossibility of combining contradictory ideas into a single construct; recall the conundrum of the square circle. As I have been arguing, however, this same logical stricture does not apply to the realm of feelings and emotions. People do experience the simultaneous push-pull of contradictory emotions. It may be a reasonable and typical experience. Yet, as has been noted, for the most part, this experience remains relatively stressful and unintegrated into experience, motivation, or action.

In this chapter, it is suggested that there is a realm of symbolic constructions in which contradictory ideas and emotions are both recognized and, for true believers, reconciled and integrated. That realm is religion. The creed, cult, and code of religious institutions have been powerful symbolic constructions throughout history. Religion has mastered the power of the symbol as a *reconciliatio oppositorum,* a synthesis of opposites. Such syntheses give great power over mind and body. This power is evident from the eastern reaches of the Mediterranean to the eastern shore of the Potomac, not to mention the erstwhile reaches of Jonestown. My purpose in this chapter is to suggest an "ambivalence hypothesis" as a speculative tool for high-

121

lighting one source of the power of religion through its ability to synthesize opposites.

It was argued above that contemporary society generates more ambivalence than it has the institutional capacity to resolve. This chapter goes back a step. Phenomenologists of religion teach that the primitive experience of the sacred is itself ambivalent. The numinous reality of the sacred is both known and mysterious, attractive and repelling, lovable and feared; it is a *mysterium* that is *tremendum, augustum, et fascinans.*

As human groups come to grips with this experience, they need to transform it into institutional rules, roles, and ideals that constitute the creed, code, and cult of believing communities. To illustrate one tradition of religious transformation, I offer an heuristic review of Western Christianity. The focus is on cognitive and structural dualisms that resolve ambivalence by symbolically combining contradictory objects into a single object of belief, e.g., infinitely powerful divinity and finitely free humanity into the divine person of Jesus. Such transformations combine antinomies of experience into one worldview and synthesize believers' contradictory emotions. The synthesis of contradictory emotions is characteristic of mythopoeic thought that is functional for believers' feeling lives.

This transformation, however, confronts contradictory processes of social life in what Thomas O'Dea (1963; 1966) called "paradoxes of institutionalization" that result in perennial sociological dilemmas. O'Dea argues that the paradoxes are particularly biting in religion. This suggests that religious institutions are essentially "double-bind institutions," at least within the Christian tradition. As a result, they generate ambivalence through both the sacred experience and the paradox of institutional imperatives. Nevertheless, religion has symbolic tools for resolving both levels of ambivalence in the true believer who then gains powerful, perhaps fanatical, motivation and security. A possible instance of this power is given in the last part of the chapter. Hopefully, this speculative essay will stimulate more research on religion, emotions, and the contemporary scene.

Religion is here interpreted as a traditional attempt at institutional resolution of disfunctional ambivalence. The resolution is effected through trans-empirical cognitive categories; emotionally charged rituals, especially at the liminal breaking points of birth, death, and rites of passage; and ethical prescriptions that absorb the tensions between law and conscience, freedom and obedience, and authority and self. Creed, cult, and code allow believers to unite the entire cosmos and personal experience into a meaningful whole (cf. Berger 1967; Luckmann 1967).

The ambivalence hypothesis leads to a definition with new emphases and strategies for the study of religion. Definitions are as good as they are usable. Ambivalence alerts us to consequences of religion in the context of the social reality of emotions. The discussion includes: the contradictory power of the sacred; apparently irreconcilable dualisms in the history of Christianity; dilemmas of institutionalized religion; and a contemporary attempt to redefine nuclear bombs as divine tools prophesied in the Bible. The last topic is part of a major paradox: in an age of rationality, science, and relativity, there is a resurgence of religious fundamentalism reaching the top political levels, even in the presumably first modern nation. I try to make sense of that development by positing ambivalence as a characteristic of modernity, and by interpreting fundamentalism as a resolution of the ambivalence.

### Ambivalence and the Sacred: Augustly Tremendous

In earlier chapters, ambivalence is briefly linked to religion in paradoxical ways. Ambivalence is interpreted both as an impetus toward "countercultural" adjustments to contemporary society, and as a reactionary response to modern threats to traditional ways of life (see Marris 1975; Yinger 1982). Furthermore, traditional religious commitment in the modern context generates ambivalence between private and public identities (Heilman 1977). There are indications that religion, at least in the Judeo-Christian traditions, is fraught with antinomies and contradictory dualisms in the nature of the Divinity, the meaning of historical events and persons, and rules for living the good life. Consider that God is the God of all, but He will slay our enemies; and that God is masculine and the God of our fathers, Abraham, Isaac, and Jacob. Original sin is the source of suffering and tragedy, yet it is a Christian *felix culpa,* happy fault, since it led God to become human. In daily living, we must be wise as serpents and gentle as doves while we lose our life in order that we may gain it by loving our neighbor as ourselves. In the end, God is love, but that love will destroy the world as we know it and punish with eternal torment those who do not follow God's will.

A traditional formula offers one link between religion and ambivalence: religious symbols provide a *reconciliatio oppositorum,* an existential synthesis of opposites within personal experience. In support of this formula, phenomenologists place ambivalence and its possible resolution at the heart of the sacred experience. Simultaneous attraction and repulsion toward the *totaliter aliter,* the totally other that is nevertheless known as sacred for me, defines believers' numinous experience. In his study of the "holy," Rudolph Otto wrote: "These two qualities, the daunting and the fascinating, now combine in a strange harmony of contrasts, and the resultant *dual character of the numinous consciousness,* ... is at once the strangest and most noteworthy phenomenon in the whole history of religion" (1923/1958: 31, italics added). Although it does not appear that Otto used ambivalence as a technical term, his words are within reach of the concept. The sacred combines the contradictory qualities of being known and mysterious, attractively fascinating and distantly august, and just too tremendous.

Ambivalent experience is explicitly noted in Van Der Leeuw's phenomenological analyses of religion. Focusing on the religious experience of awe and the forces of love and power, he states that "because these attitudes show two main tendencies, one away from Power and the other toward it, we speak of the *ambivalent* nature of awe" (1933/1963: 47–8, his italics; see Wheelwright 1968, for an aesthetic interpretation of the "tensive" ambivalence of "awe"). Van Der Leeuw interprets contradiction at the heart of sacred love as the foundation of religious experience: "Love in the religious sense, ... never exists wholly free from its apparent opponent, fear. ... This *ambivalent* experience of love may even be regarded as the *basic* experience in religion..." (1933/1963: 509, italics added).

This statement generalizes Otto's discussion of contradictory emotions toward the sacred by placing ambivalent awe at the heart of religious experience. As social analysts argue, religious ritual both allays existential anxiety and generates religious anxiety. So too, religious experience of the sacred may allay existential ambivalence and generate its own kind. In this process, religion accomplishes its essential functions of devaluing mundane realities as mere ephemera, and of constructing an aura of transcendent reality around its own objects. The transformation is made real within worshippers' feelings. The core of personal being is seen to be a spirit transformed into an instance of divine power and love that answers or, better, devalues mundane woes and stretches self on the salvific tension of religious ambivalence.

More recently, Weston La Barre interprets this salvific tension by extending the Freudian model of ambivalent identification of son with father to all morality and religion. He sees religion as a projected reality reflected from the dynamics of personality development. An important function of religion as projection is to resolve the ambivalence at the center of self and its formative relationships. La Barre states bluntly: "Ambivalence is the hallmark of all religion and morality" (1972: 375). It characterizes religious and moral experience. Peter Berger puts modern ambivalence in the sacred tension within the individual between the total otherness of the Divinity and Its presence within one's own self (1980: 42). He mentions mysticism as an oft-tried though difficult solution. Institutionalized religion is, in part, a functional transformation of that experience and retains its contradictory strains.

Something like the ambivalence of the sacred is found in ritualized and quasi-religious experiences of personal relationships. For example, Eisenstadt and Roniger (1984), in a suggestive study, analyze the feelings and understandings of solidarity among "patrons, clients, and friends." They find that an essential aspect of such relationships is ambivalence between the "spiritual" ties of intimacy and the concrete institutionalized duties that such ties entail; between kinship relations and the bonds of friendship; between instrumental institutional ties and expressive interpersonal bonds; and, in general, following Victor Turner's work, between social structure and communitas via the ambivalent state of liminality. They see ambivalence generated by the unavoidable co-existence of these aspects of relationships that combine contradictory yet complementary feelings, definitions, and expectations. Relationships are desired and functional, yet they generate stress and conflict. This discussion leads to a dialectical model of human relationships shot through with ambivalence.

As a response to the sacred, institutionalized religion helps believers overcome primordial ambivalence by grasping it cognitively through myth and dogma; controlling it affectively through rituals and rules synthesizing mixed emotions; acting it out according to meaningful prescriptions governing mundane action; and thus, eventually reconciling cultural contradictions within individual experience. This reconciliation is the applied task of *cura animarum*, the care of souls, through practical religious intelligence giving motivation and direction to everyday life: the content of the Sunday homily smooths wrinkled consciences and allows business as usual on Monday. Consequences of institutionalized religion present believers as well as ecclesiastics with additional dilemmas that can generate a kind of secondary ambivalence even within an overarching total interpretation. The religious "sacred canopy" (Berger 1967), however, remains a powerful ambivalence-resolving possibility for moderns, even in secular culture.

The primordial ambivalence of the sacred and the institutionalized ambivalence of religion suggest a definition of religion. Using ambivalence to interpret religion as both an experiential phenomenon and a functioning institution, we state that: religion refers to *those institutionalized modes of behavior, feeling rules, and sets of intentionalities by which humans contain ambivalence within a symbolic order that ultimately reconciles opposites.* This definition combines aspects of functional, substantive, symbolic, and political standpoints (cf. Anthony and Robbins 1975; Bellah 1975; Berger 1967; 1974; Luckmann 1967). The synthesis of opposites is what only symbols can do, and religious symbols are powerful, wide-ranging, and ultimate. They realign conflicting emotions and release powerful motivation for action. The next section takes a heuristic look at contradictory motifs in Western Christianity. Then the discussion moves to the general dilemmas of institutionalizing sacred experience in religious organizations.

## *Ambivalence and Christianity: The Human God*

Selected oppositions in Western Christianity can be interpreted as sources of ambivalence and linked with simple models of social organization (Bellah 1964). For example, Judeo-Grecian cultural dualisms include: chosen people and gentiles; Yahweh and Baalim; Hellenae and barbaroi; form and matter; one and the many; appearances and essence; and the moral categories of good and evil, happy and unhappy. With Christianity came sin and grace; heaven and hell; One and Triune; in and outside the Church; nature and supernature; and the tormenting division between the saved and the damned. These formulations structured the everyday lives of the people (cf. Gouldner 1975).

In the West, these dualisms were framed and cathected on a "we-they" division with the person located within a group in a horizontally dichotomized context versus other groups (see Table 1). This nexus turned into an objective, metaphysical, and supernatural frame in the Christian era with the dualistic interpretation of the individual in a vertially stratified and polarized society of nobles and serfs. Ambivalent experiences are objectified and attributed to real forces "out there." Conflicting feelings are interpreted in the available vocabulary and worldview, e.g., as a real "temptation" by the Devil or actual "grace" from God. In resisting temptation, the person is fighting real forces and beings who are causing the conflict within one's experience.

With the disenchantment of the Western world; the demythologization of consciousness; and the rise of modernity, there developed the existential subjective sense that renders dualisms "out there" less plausible. Luther sought Christ "for me" and shifted the emphasis to personal experience of salvation. Eventually, Freud, for example, located felt dualisms "in here" with Eros and Thanatos; anthropologists taught that conscious structures are relative to cultural definitions (cf. Douglas 1989); sociologists argue that experience of transcendent or immanent religious realities is internalized from social forces (cf. Swanson, 1967). Mass communication; increased geographical and psychic mobility; and urbanism and cosmopolitanism as ways of life foster perspectival theories of truth that was previously seen "naturally" in relation to external forces. The sources of felt conflict are now no longer projected onto natural or supernatural causes or beings; they are seen as conventional effects of human action and definition.

There is a suggestive parallelism between the development of Western consciousness and the resolution of ambivalent feelings in the Christian tradition. The development of Christianity from a quasi-tribal messianism to the religion of the early city and empire and to the dominant force in Medieval Europe is well known. Within this movement came modes of thought from the quasi-tribal and personal biography of the kerygmatic Christ; to the teaching and catechesis of the early Christian community; to the cosmic symbolism of the Greek Fathers; to the incipient scholasticism of the first Church councils and the neo-Platonism of Augustine; and finally to the Aristotelian syntheses of Aquinas and later systematic scholasticism.

The scholastic framework carried into the twentieth century as the context for Catholic thought, while Protestant thinkers stayed closer to philosophical and historical developments. The contemporary scene finds frameworks vying

## Table 1
## Typology of Traditional Binary Models* of Ambivalence

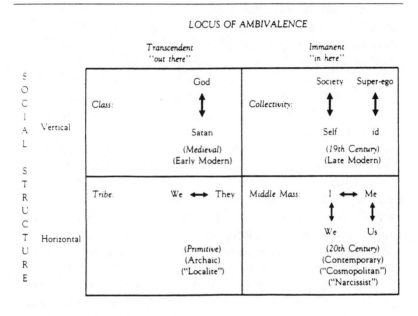

*See Bellah 1964.

for dominance as Catholic thought meets Marxism in liberation theology; the longer Christian tradition is appreciated by Protestant thinkers; and Evangelical and Fundamentalist groups grow stronger even as new religious movements emerge or are imported from the East. Tradition-faith-rationality conflicts continue within modern experience.

A somewhat parallel development can be suggested for liturgical practices from the Judeo and folk elements in the agape of early Christian communities to the gradually routinized forms of the Roman Latin Mass and the common devotions stylized by the time of the Reformation. Protestant liturgical varieties developed thereafter, while the Catholic Mass remained fixed until the reforms of Vatican II in the 1960s. The current scene offers a variety of liturgical practices within and across denominations and reborn charismatic forms (cf. Hesser and Weigert 1980). Liturgies lose awe as mysterious tongues give way to the mundane meanings of natural talk characteristic of Christianity in its origins. Contemporary liturgies are communitarian with settings that emphasize subjective this-worldly meaning rather than objective transcendent reference. Moderns seek to feel good and find God rather than do good and avoid hell.

This sketch portrays different institutionalizations of dualities within a symbolic order, i.e., a culture. The earlier stages represented in Table 1 are characterized by the *"part-icipative"* symbol or myth wherein subjective expressiveness is dominant, though objective representativeness is also "seen" (see Langer 1958). It is the consciousness of the quasi-tribal community. Ambivalence is resolved in terms of one's collective identity within the group. The symbol for early Christians is the cross with the corpus of Jesus the Christ, which can be interpreted as the totem God/man of the group. Individuals come to be interpreted as *real parts* of the group or "mystical body."

By contrast, the Medieval stage is characterized by the *"projected"* symbol wherein objective representativeness is dominant, though expressiveness is also felt. Ambivalence is resolved in terms of the reality "out there." Dominant symbols are the lofty ascent of Gothic cathedrals *pro*duced by the community to represent and to "be" its place in the hierarchical universe. God and humans are in a tense, vertically polarized, cosmic as well as legal equilibrium of the Communion of Saints.

Up to the Reformation, it could be hypothesized that Western Christianity absorbed ambivalence by physical objects that were also symbols of realities that are "supernatural" and external to the material and cultural order. God, Satan, angels, heaven, hell, purgatory, or limbo are really "out there" as metaphysical realities rendered apparent by the objects and groups which carried them, whether it is the religio-political structure of a regal centralized *Respublica Christiana,* the witnessing community of grandly housed monks or nuns, or the worshipping group assembled in the cathedral.

From the Reformation and Luther's illuminating ques-

tion, "Who is Christ for me?" however, the locus of ambivalence shifted to the interior life mediated through the word
of a newly translated Scripture, although the forces are still
symbolized as from outside. The battleground is the conscience of individuals agonizing over the questions, "Am I
saved"? "How do I know"? (cf. Weber 1958). The Protestant
symbol becomes the vernacular text of the Bible through
which the word of God guides the ambivalent individual
who alone, whether really predestined or not, is subjective-
ly responsible for his or her soul. Against this personaliza-
tion of the salvation question, the Catholic tradition held to
institutional forms and public sacraments signaling an
external, hierarchical, and legal solution to felt ambivalence.

   The point-counterpoint of dogma-heresy depicts sociological ambivalence at the organizational level within the
Christian tradition. In a dialectical study of the modernist
controversy in the Catholic Church toward the end of the
last century, Lester Kurtz (1986) uses sociological ambivalence as an interpretive tool. He describes the modernist
crisis as the breakdown of traditional Roman Catholic solutions to the contradictory demands of independent scholar-
ship versus obedience to hierarchical authority. Protagonists in each camp originally identify themselves as loyal to
the Catholic Church, and yet they experience the ambivalence of contradictory norms in intricately related status
sets such as scholar-priest, or researcher-monk.

   Kurtz discusses sources of ambivalence and suggests
possible solutions (see chap. 3). He notes that ambivalence
can be functional for individual growth and institutional
adaptation, but if it reaches a critical point re-enforced by
conflicting significant others and hierarchical opposition,
then ambivalence becomes disfunctional for the individual,
the institution, or both. Crisis results. Individuals try to
resolve ambivalence by eliminating one set of contradictory
norms, either socially by giving up membership in one
group or epistemically by ceasing to believe in one set of
norms. The institution, meanwhile, can reform its norms,
relax demands for behavioral conformity, or in the short
run, expel the rebel.

Kurtz's study highlights two points: for believers, a religious worldview can function to eliminate ambivalence; and religion as a social institution can generate secondary ambivalence among believers who are also members of institutions with contradictory norms. His study supports the further hypothesis that reactions to ambivalence tend to become amplified; that is, ambivalent actors eventually over-react so that ecclesiastics bitterly persecute "heretics," and those persecuted bitterly attack each other and the ecclesiastics.

In spite of ecclesiastical objections, however, cultural contradictions continue. Sartre, for example, nicely captures contemporary ambivalence in the contradictory dictum that we are "condemned to be free." Camus gives us the image of endlessly pushing a rock up a hill to grasp the contradictory quest for clarity in confrontation with the stubborn opaqueness of existence: the absurd in an age of rationality. With no cognitive certainty "out there," moderns turn on an "in here" dimension seeking relationships that are emotionally meaningful and secure. The modern is aware of the relativity of cultural norms; of the hypothetical nature of scientific models of the universe; of the threatening movement of socio-political and environmental events; and of mass culture that weakens the inner self searching for identity (cf. Baumeister 1986; Klapp 1969; Weigert et al. 1986).

For many, the 1960s buried the transcendent audience out there. The "Honest to God," "Secular City," and "God is dead" theses promulgated the Nietzschian announcement of the death of the vertically projected Other who could resolve ambivalence. Transitoriness is felt in the absence of an unchanging God to ground stable feelings. The traditional religious self is not plausible without a Significant Other and Divine Namegiver who bestows and validates personal identity beyond reach of worm, rot, or the wrecking ball (cf. Bellah 1968). Peer play and narcissistic fulfillment rise in intensity (Lasch 1979). These meanings, however, are obviously human constructions and cannot synthesize the oppositions of experience. The horizontal confrontation of ambivalence now results in perduring anxiety. As Sartre saw, "Hell is the other." Yet, salvation, the felt meaningful synthesis of the oppositions in our lives, remains the perennial religious task.

Moderns live within or between the cosmic certainty of sectarian groups and the acosmic uncertainty of transitory situational meanings. Narcissism is one response; belligerent nationalism, political martyrdom, terrorist fanaticism, or dogmatic fundamentalist movements of the left or right are others (see Glock and Bellah 1976). Ambivalence guarantees the relevance of religion in spite of, and indeed our hypothesis suggests, because of relativistic rationality. Institutions both resolve primary ambivalence and generate sociological ambivalence. The dilemma also applies to religious institutions that try to tame the sacred.

## *Dilemmas of Institutionalized Religion: Spirit or Letter?*

To be socially real, charismatic experience must be made available on everyday terms for ordinary folk. Max Weber spoke of the "routinization," or "everydayness," of charisma as a fundamental sociological process. The most moving experience is socially stillborn if it is not reproduced for subsequent generations and made part of the community's way of life. The same goes for the sacred experience, but the paradox of routinization is magnified in the souls of believers and in the minds of liturgists and theologians. A sentiment attributed to the fiery evangelist Billy Sunday captures this tension. It runs something like this: I know as much about theology as a jackrabbit knows about Ping Pong, but I'm on my way to glory. Theology is essential for passing down Sunday's glory ride, but experiencing the ride may be irrelevant to the hard-hearted theologian.

Thomas O'Dea (1963; 1966) focussed on the paradoxical process of institutionalization. Religious experience is ecstatic, liminal, mysterious, uncanny—and many other breakthrough adjectives that fly in the face of routine, mundane, everyday ennui. Yet, established religions are institutions facing mundane imperatives and functional necessities similar to other organizations. How can religions both grasp and reproduce the founding experience? Religious experience says extraordinary, ecstatic; religious institution says ordinary, mundane. Religious believers face the dilemma of living a sacred experience in the midst of routine reality; religious practitioners face the dilemma of performing routine rituals with religious motivation. If religious experience of the sacred is a charismatic breakthrough of the divine into the mundane world, how can mundane activity reproduce and embody that divine experience without destroying it? The most ecstatic religious experience has to be packaged with the same social stuff as any other human phenomenon. The inner *sanctum* is still made of silk and stone and symbols.

In his sociological reflections, O'Dea posits five paradoxes or dilemmas at different moments in the institutionalization process: mixed motivation; objectifying symbols versus alienation from the symbol process; elaborated bureaucracy and administrative alienation; vital concrete definitions versus the letter killing the spirit; and the power issue of voluntarism versus conformity. These moments cover a range of analysis: motivation; the relationship of individual and institution; and cultural symbols. Let us touch each dilemma in turn.

First-generation members in a religious movement are "converted followers" of a charismatic leader, a person who embodies a break with traditional meanings and yet fuses them into new motivation that answers disciple's deepest needs. They, in turn, are so fired as to follow their leader in a new way of life even unto death. Giving up previous identities; sacrificing known routines of daily life; and suffering martyrdom to witness their new-found faith, first-generation believers experience the power of other-worldly, mundanely disinterested motives that turn the workaday world upside down.

With the organizational task of reproducing itself as the accepted faith of generations of "born members," and with the effect of rational imperatives toward specialization and bureaucratization, religious institutions, at least in Western societies, undergo a formalization of offices and identities. This process effects a transformation of institutional goals.

Leaders become clergy and vie for influence and power. They ensconce themselves as, for example, bishops who are princes and warriors, or more recently, hierarchs and corporate bureaucrats. The motivation of such leaders is scarcely distinguishable from executives in other social institutions, and the motivation of the membership is statistically akin to other traditional and "comforting" institutions. The otherworldly, disinterested, self-sacrificing motivation of the charismatic generation is replaced by functioning, thisworldly, and quite interested motivation of well-established religious leaders and well-heeled religious believers.

The second dilemma concerns reproducing the founding experiences of the sacred. The vehicles of reproduction are the same as those that carry other social meanings: rules, rituals, and symbols. The power of ritual for reproducing religious meaning remains precarious. As O'Dea (1966: 93) notes, "The embodiment of the sacred in the profane vehicle causes a loss of sacredness." Believers, however, have no other social means at hand. Cultic pathos follows as "repetition robs ritual of . . . charisma, and routinizes it." As a result, the cultic symbols and rituals lose their vital power as worshippers are no longer able to cultivate those "things" and to invest them with psychic energy (cf. Rochberg-Halton 1986). The symbols become unintelligible, unevocative, dead; in a word, they become alien, and worshippers become alienated. Rituals no longer resonate with reproduced religious experience. The history of religions shows a certain periodization of alienation that leads to protest: iconoclasts; radical Protestant reforms; disputes over hymns; dead mystical versus live vernacular languages; and concern for liturgical relevance are manifestations of the symbolic dilemma that stretches believers from live traditions to dead symbols.

The third dilemma focuses on organizational processes. The formal organization and bureaucratization of religious institutions involve the formation of hierarchical offices and standard procedures for solving problems. The sacred nature of religious institutions informs these historically contingent solutions with awesome power, legitimacy, and conservative strength. Historical change, both within and without what we may now call churches, demands the continual modification or elimination of older institutional forms and the construction of new ones. To the extent that the identities of officeholders is alienated from the founding experience and from the everyday experience of members, we have a religious institution with an over-elaborated structure that is ineffective in transmitting the original charism, and a class of clerical leaders that is alienated both from the crucial issues of the time and from the religious needs of its members. Yet, the institutionalized church is heavily identified with and in great need of its administrators and hierarchs, even if they become increasingly alienated, alienating, and irrelevant.

The fourth dilemma concerns the unavoidable necessity of effective definitions and interpretations to pass on the religious message and its ethical, credal, and affective uses. New converts and succeeding generations want to learn what the religious message is all about: what to do; what to believe; and how to handle life's crises. The religious institution's ethical message evolves from casuistry to rules to a code of ethics and finally to a style of life that distinguishes the saved from the damned, or those who belong to the believing community from those who do not.

The conviction for regulating one's way of life comes in part from shared beliefs that need to be protected from contradictory, conflicting, and heretical interpretations. So the faith life of the community develops from commitment to a charismatic person to belief in the stories and assent to the propositions made about that life and its meaning. Belief moves from belief in a Saviour to belief in statements about the Saviour. Finally, material symbols of the original message become mere means to feeling secure and knowing the answer: symbols become mechanized, e.g., sacred things become good luck charms; prayers become magical formulae; and original stories become literal statements about current and future events as canonized texts are translated into historical laws and apocalyptic prophecies. Mechanization of symbols attempts to answer the ambivalence believers feel in the face of the Pauline insistence on faith while facing the realization that "the letter killeth, but the spirit giveth life" (O'Dea 1966: 94).

The final dilemma concerns social power. Believers confront the push-pull of faith versus doubt; religious leaders face the dilemma of fidelity to the original religious call and success in the larger society. The religious institution is torn between fidelity to God and loyalty to Caesar; between transcendent yearnings and the mundane demands of success; between conventional conformity and the uncomfortable call to holiness and prophetic critique. Institutionalization brings altar and throne, church and state, human aspirations and national identity into periods of uneasy alliance and lethal conflict. In the Constintinian era, Christian altars and pagan thrones were aligned; in the age of Aquarius, they are split and pulling against not only themselves but other universalistic religions as well. Religion remains ambivalent to the seduction of power in its relationship with the dominant society and to the prophetic costs of power from its faith commitments. The same, on lower frequencies, remains for the faith-doubt, conformity-criticism ambivalence of individual believers.

The contemporary world witnesses the conflict of theocracies, *Kulturreligionen,* and quasi-religious ideologies in the dilemmas of East-West, North-South, Centralized-Ethnic, Developed-Developing societies. Indeed, the dilemmas of religious institutions are the dilemmas of institutions generally. The next section offers a speculative application of the ambivalence hypothesis to a numinous object newly on the scene.

*An Instance of Religion Taming Ambivalence:*
*Eschatologizing the "Bomb"*

Beliefs about the origin and destiny of the world are touchstone religious issues. Traditional beliefs in a universe created and governed by a providential God are contradicted by physical models beginning in a Big Bang and heading for cold entropy with no tolerance for human life. The creationism-science debate goes on while unimaginable power over nature is put at the disposal of short-term interests. Humans are, for the first time, responsible for the earth at the systemic level that supports their own species life. This great new responsibility is symbolized by the nuclear arms danger, or emblematically, the "Bomb."

The Bomb brings together two conflicting interpretive frames, the natural and the social (see Goffman 1974; Johnson and Weigert 1980). There appears to be a profound historical reversal in the contemporary perception of nature. In primitive worldviews, nature was often perceived as a fearful power to be placated by magic. With the transition from Babylonian to Greek science, nature was seen as a dangerous machine whose workings are explained by theoretical reconstructions. The Judeo-Christian vision saw nature as the field of God's eternal law and the outcome of God's power, as *vestigia Dei*. In idealistic Enlightenment optimism, nature was benign and malleable, once reason controls disease, chemical processes, and meteorological patterns. In this Century, however, there is a reversal of belief in progress. The reversal is indelibly graven in the trenches of the Somme and the images of Hiroshima and Nagasaki.

This shift is paralleled by Christian eschatological beliefs exemplified in the best selling book in the U.S. during the 1970s, *The Late Great Planet Earth* (Lindsey 1977). Historically, Christian eschatology began with apparently literal belief in cosmic events, such as stars falling and fire consuming while war between good and evil purified the earth for God's Kingdom. Gradually, eschatology developed into an existential and moral understanding with no literal application to the history or future of the earth (Barkun 1983; Hoekema 1979). Demythologized eschatology came to dominate mainline Christian thought, while Fundamentalist groups kept a literal apocalyptic version.

The real images of the nuclear age warrant a stunning reversal. In the post-Hiroshima age, the cosmic literalness of Fundamentalist Protestant eschatology takes on greater plausibility than the mildly optimistic demythologized versions: the apocalyptic Book of Revelation read literally appears more applicable to the current scene than liberal metaphoric renditions. Cosmic devastation now appears more likely than widespread moral conversion. In a further ironic turn, secular scientific thinkers fashion eschatologies parallel to the predictions of their ideological foes, the Biblical literalists: both see the earth likely to be destroyed in fire and darkness (Barkun 1985; Schell 1982). In a nuclear age, engines of progress are unmasked as engines of destruction, and humans, not gods, are driving those engines.

The nuclear age involves a shift in the interpretation of nature from a natural to a social frame in which humans are responsible for their physical future. Interpretations of nature today do not lead to shared magical rituals placating cosmic powers nor to a common religion imploring divine persons, but to socio-political maneuvering and ideological conflict. Ignorant warring societies have no universal myth for synthesizing the ambivalent self-nature relationship. Such synthesis may be impossible within a social frame in which negotiation entrains destiny.

There are ambivalent pressures also from the self-society relationship. The tension between instrumental individualism, or "What's in it for me?" and commitment to the collectivity, or "What can I do for us?" grinds sharper than ever. Split feelings over the direction of social relations create uncertain responses but certain anxiety. Contemporary psychologizing of institutional effects blinds us to larger social processes. As Wexler (1983) argues, personal dilemmas must be linked to structural contradictions if we are to understand the self-society relationship and not end with the misdirected question, "What's wrong with *me?*" As a speculative application, we briefly examine one source of contemporary ambivalence and a religious resolution of one of today's master questions, How do I live with the Bomb?

The Bomb is complex. There are good reasons for having nuclear arms and there are good reasons for abandoning them. There are no only good reasons for using them. Moderns are caught in a nuclear dilemma reflected across the ideological spectrum. The fear is immediate: 34.6% of American college students expect nuclear war in their lifetime (Chronicle 1986), and 31.5% of Britains aged 18–24 expect nuclear war before the year 2000 (Jowell et al. 1986). Moderns both need the Bomb and reject it; find it both awesome and fearsome; both are excited and revulsed by it—the phenomenology of the sacred reflected in Oppenheimer's religious language about creating and destroying worlds upon witnessing the first awesome cloud.

Moderns need a symbolic transformation to reconcile themselves with the Bomb, as with any ambivalence-generating object. Consider a Fundamentalist transformation of nuclear threat into characteristic religious certainty:

> God warns us . . . the *day of reckoning* is here! World War III will *start* with nuclear devastation unleashed on London, Birmingham, Manchester, Liverpool, New York, Washington . . . ! But if *you* . . . make it an UNCONDITIONAL surrender . . . through the living Jesus Christ as personal Savior—then NO PLAGUE shall come near you! Those in the true Body of Christ shall be taken to a place of SAFETY. . . .
> (Armstrong 1980: 183–4, italics his)

Fear is transmogrified into desire: my salvation on earth. The worst ushers in the best. "As the battle of Armageddon reaches its awful climax and its appears that all life will be destroyed on earth—in this very moment Jesus Christ will return and save man from self-extinction . . ." (Lindsey 1977: 156–7).

Religion can transform threatening weapons into means and portents of salvation. A national poll finds that ca. 39% of Americans believe that the Bible tells us about nuclear war when it "predicts that the earth will be destroyed by fire" (Public Agenda Foundation 1984). Such widespread Biblical literalism reflects a yearning for resolving the nuclear situation and an ambivalence that is hypothesized to be part of that yearning. Furthermore, religiously oriented respondents most likely agree that the U.S.S.R. is an "evil empire" with whom the U.S. will go to war, but against empirical predictions, respondents believe that faith in God will ensure their survival anyway (Yankelovich and Doble 1984). Here are intriguing relationships among beliefs, ambivalent feelings, and the nuclear situation!

Two journalistic investigations echo these relationships in the talk of believers. Religious solutions often combine starkly held but apparently contradictory beliefs. This is the religious paradox made vivid in Max Weber's wonder how Calvinists' belief in predestination could provide motivation to work incessantly to succeed in earning daily bread and more. An analogous question is: how can individuals who believe that nuclear devastation literally predicted by God is immanent also feel certain as they buy insurance and plan vacations that they will be spared from Armageddon? What answers absorb nuclear ambivalence and transform it into secure futures?

Traveling with Fundamentalist Christians in the Holy Land, Grace Halsell (1986) heard her companion, Clyde, explain that he believes Ezekiel's prophecy of earth's destruction in Armageddon. "Ezekiel could scarcely have been referring to anything other than an exchange of tactical nuclear weapons" (25–6). He concluded that "all history has in a sense been predetermined by God. . . . So, in the great final battle God will again take charge of human history" (27). Is Clyde frightened by the prediction of nuclear war? Does he want the world to end? Yes and No. He will be saved because he believes, but loved ones and innocents will be lost because they do not believe.

Believers anticipate empirical safety in the midst of nuclear catastrophe. Clyde believes he will be saved by Rapture: "I'm driving with my friend who is not saved, and the Rapture occurs, which, again, I expect any day, and I'm lifted up in the air out of the car. The car runs amok. And my friend is killed in the crash. . . . I rejoice in the idea of meeting my Savior" (Halsell 1986: 37). Once saved, believers' concern over loved ones, another source of ambivalence, ends. Clyde adds, "The agony of friends and loved ones in hell will be entirely deleted from the mind of the survivors in heaven" (37). The dire empirical prediction is transformed into the singleminded joy of salvation.

In another firsthand account, A. G. Mojtabai was drawn to Amarillo, Texas by the awe of Pantex, the final assembly plant for all nuclear weapons in the U.S., and by the wonder how ordinary townspeople grasp the paradox of "a pastoral of cows browsing around the perimeter of the plant" (1986: 66). She studied the people and place for four years and finally moved there. She found that people put the thought of assembling earth-destroying weapons just out of town further out of their minds, but they also retain a deep sense of ambivalence. Mojtabai devoted a chapter to their divided attitudes toward: artifacts; view of the future; self-perception as Frontiersmen; and current issues (212–3).

As a secular thinker, she was surprised that religious beliefs about the future dominate Amarillan's schema for absorbing the contradictions they feel. Their view of the future is dominated by two kinds of American exceptionalism: technological progress and Fundamentalist eschatology, or what she calls "End Time" thinking. The situation generates ambivalence evident in interviews with civic leaders and Pantex workers. As she writes, "When someone stands a few miles from Pantex . . . and declares: 'We are the terminal generation,' that assertion has a resonance it might not have elsewhere" (xi). Some live with the ambivalence; others become numb to it; and some absorb it in an eschatology of "blessed assurance."

She found that the linchpin End Time belief is Rapture, "the divine rescue of true believers from the coming holocaust" (xi). This is the key for solving existential dilemmas concerning the End. Rapture ensures believers' physical safety and is the sure sign of salvation. A survey of Southern Baptist ministers corroborates belief in Rapture as a powerful correlate of this type of End Time thinking (Turner and Guth 1988). We know no national statistic on belief in Rapture. The sale's of Rapturist literature and the likelihood that some of the 39% of Americans who believe the Bible predicts nuclear war also believe in Rapture suggests that many millions interpret the Bomb with a synthesis of empirical expectations and supernatural events. Mere human action cannot stop Armageddon, but believing in Jesus will save us from its devastation.

In a careful firsthand study of Southside Gospel Church, Nancy Ammerman (1987) finds Rapture a pervasive belief that "produces a sense of impending doom" (157). The pastor of the church translates the nuclear situation into a motive for religious fear: "If we fear the bomb, how much more we ought to fear God's judgment" (157). Yet, if we are saved, we should yearn for release from this world that is so evil that it simply must be ended soon. Believers expect the Lord's quick return. One woman commented, "How much worse can it get? He promised it, didn't he?" (45). As a young member made clear:

> I'm looking for the Rapture. I mean this world is getting so bad that I won't read a newspaper.... My brother and I were discussing how close the Rapture is, how near it is. He was saying "I'm really looking forward to it because it is just so bad that I almost can't stand it any more" (46).

These words reflect the motif of this chapter: modern dynamics generate ambivalent situations; and religion offers effective ambivalence-resolving beliefs, rituals, and communities.

## Summary

This chapter brings together a sociological approach to religion through the concept of ambivalence. I believe that it is a necessary concept for grasping contemporary emotions and enlarging the social scientific analysis of religion. These are speculative steps. They lead to an ambivalence-religion hypothesis that appears fruitful in a selective review of Western Christianity, religious institutionalization, and a brief application to Fundamentalist apocalypticism, namely, End Time thinking and the Bomb.

This is a first word. Ambivalence may be posited as a primordial experience, or analyzed as the result of sociocultural forces. The pluralism and contradictions of today's world are generating more ambivalence than social institutions can resolve. This leads to a consideration of religion as a traditional ambivalence-resolving institution through its function of combining conceptual and emotional polarities into totalized worldviews. Phenomenological and psychoanalytic scholars find ambivalence at the heart of the religious experience. A fruitful definition of religion can be formulated around its ambivalence-resolving function.

With an eye on the hypothetical payoff of this definition, a contemporary and speculative application is made to anticipation of nuclear war and religious resolutions to the ambivalence felt toward the Bomb. Indications of such ambivalence are found in survey, interview, and observational data. The hypothesis is that distressful ambivalence toward the Bomb strengthens Fundamentalist eschatology in the midst of rational secular culture, a strength that reverses the main historical direction of Christian eschatology away from belief in cosmic events.

Fundamentalist apocalypticism is vividly presented in Hal Lindsey's books. Apocalyptic thinking can be interpreted as support for the ambivalence-religion hypothesis. It remains for others systematically to test this against alternative interpretations. We must come to grips with the cognitive and emotional experience of ambivalence toward a contradictory world of increasing technological progress and increasingly absurd technological violence (cf. Lifton 1976; Lifton and Falk 1982). I am certain that ambivalence and its resolution are definitive features of religion today.

# Chapter 6

☐

# Ambivalence:
# The Temper of Modernity?

This final chapter is divided into four parts. First, a brief extension of the main line of thought is offered. Second, I present selected hypotheses that underwrite the argument that is clearly speculative at many points. Third, a few suggestions are made for interpreting modern life. After this, I look at a few general ways in which scholars deepen our understanding of ambivalence.

*Recapitulation: How Did We Get This Far?*

The story of ambivalence covered a bit of ground, chronologically and analytically, with focus on the latter. Since the term was coined at the turn of the century, its relevance to understanding twentieth-century life is symbolized by the context of its appearance—at the start of our century and in the psychological explanation of modern experience. I briefly traced the emergence of ambivalence as a technical term and folk category. As the word spread and persons learn to think of themselves as ambivalent, this modern construct is deemed essential to self-understanding and cultural analysis. The remaining pages offer concluding reflections on where we may go from here.

The modern context generates ambivalence as a paradox of increasing short-run freedom toward, control over,
and responsibility for nature, society, and self. Concomi-
tantly, the possibility for long-run destruction of nature,
society, and self grows. That is one of our working themes.
There are historical shifts in mentality: from a natural or
supernatural "frame" to a social frame in which humans
alone are the responsible agents. It is as though Comte's
assertion over a century ago has become today's cliche:
theological, philosophical, and positivistic attitudes succeeded each other, and yet they continue to fight for control
over modern minds and collective action.

Interpreting accounts Americans use to make moral
sense out of their lives, Bellah et al. (1985) list contradictory pulls on the core value, individualism. The lode vein is
autonomy and self-reliance at almost all costs, yet Americans realize that life makes sense only if shared in intimacy
and community; life's chances are grasped by those with
advantages, supposedly talent and motivation, but real life
gives the edge to privileged birth and wealth while society
grows more unequal in security and dignity. Living together
demands realistic give and take, yet moral compromise is
condemned. In the end, Bellah et al. conclude that the
"inner tensions of American individualism add up to a clas-
sic case of ambivalence" (150–1). These words echo
Baumeister's suggestion that modern ambivalence is "the
desire to make commitments versus the desire not to give
up any options . . ."(1986: 232). In a bold generalization within a framework including both the evolution of the species
and the development of the individual, Robert Kegan (1982)
posits fundamental ambivalence between forces and yearnings for independence and inclusion; toward autonomous
individuality and heteronomous collectivity.

Evidence for increasing ambivalence comes from studies of the bureaucratic personality. Williams et al. (1980)
argue that we must take account of the "hidden arrangements" of bureaucratic organizations as well as the public
rules. With rapid change in ownership, personnel, and

clients, the bureaucratic person may experience "social paranoia." Paranoia is a reasonable response to contradictory demands both from particularistic norms that bind subjects to be loyal to superiors, and from threatening shifts in power that treat subjects as pawns with no entitlement to status. Double-bind messages from superiors are punctuated with degradation ceremonies like a "donkey barbecue," in which a superior publicly humiliates a supposedly loyal subordinate to dramatize the superior's control over employees' fate and feelings. By analogy with the Mertonian doctor, we speak of the functionality of subordinates' donkey experience of a contradictory emotion, "detached loyalty." I heard a phrase that captures this bureaucratic ambivalence, "I'm loyal, but I'm not a jerk." Such may be the appropriate response for anyone in a discrepant role generating loyalties divided along the fault lines of conflicting demands (cf. Goffman 1959).

Arlie Hochschild's (1983) analysis of occupations involving emotional labor shows that managing ambivalence is imperative in a service-oriented economy. Larger percentages of growing occupations, e.g., professions, services, sales, etc, produce an emotional product along with whatever else is produced. She notes that approximately twice as many women as men work these jobs, thus placing emotional labor on women's shoulders, or smiles. She compares flight attendants who work mainly face to face to produce positive feelings, and bill collectors who work mainly phone to phone to foster fear. Each manipulates the feeling rules that tell us what to feel and when, like pleasure on the plane or fear on the phone.

What happens if the person does not *feel* the appropriate emotion? As an offering to others or to the rule-makers, the laborer may *pretend* to feel the emotion. Pretense feigned time after time demands skilled acting if the desired definition of the situation is to be sustained and participant's identity is to survive. Hochschild distinguishes two methods of acting: surface and deep. Surface acting demands only that the performer manage the body so that the audience understands what is communicated: the classically arched eyebrow communicates skeptical scrutiny while the performer feels nothing of the sort. Deep acting, made popular by young Marlon Brando, demands that the performer communicate from one's inner self to the inner selves of the audience. The performer feels the proper emotion supposedly resulting from the surface performance, or manages cognitive and emotional processes such that the appropriate feeling is experienced, even though it may result from images that have nothing to do with the situation at hand. The latter type is easier to realize; it is the "method acting" of Stanislavski. According to Hochschild, method acting becomes another dramaturgical skill required in those businesses that produce positive feelings as one of their products. As Goffman said, moderns must be skilled in the arts of stagecraft (1959).

Although Hochschild does not use ambivalence as an organizing concept, the term reappears as she discusses: a young woman struggling to define her guilty attraction for an older priest (44–5); an anxious bride marching down the aisle in what is supposed to be unglossed joy (61); stressed and vaguely guilty men, and especially women, at the death of a parent (65–6); the time and place of expressions of grief (67–8); and the pride cum envy of a woman who is "only" a housewife (82–3). In emotional labor, contradictory feelings become part of the job and its product. Workers, nevertheless, often resent putting personal feelings up for public consumption by the corporation's clients (90, passim).

Commercialization of feelings leads to a deep contradiction between what the person feels and what emotional production requires that person to do. Divisions between deep feelings and the surface self results in "feigning rather than feeling." Repeated feigning generates self-estrangement. Ambivalence comes to characterize the person's relationship to self, as well as to the client and the job. This is Goffman's dramaturgical ambivalence toward the performed self felt with an alienated vengeance.

For those who resolve the division by identifying with the job, burnout is likely, while those who reject the job face feelings of hypocrisy, frustration, and cynicism. Others try to keep a balance between spontaneity or impulse and the institutional demands (cf. Turner 1976; 1978 and person-role merger).

Analysis of the relationship between a sense of self and publicly defined identities allows us to extend Goffman's discussion of stigma mentioned earlier. He states, "Given that the stigmatized individual in our society acquires identity standards which he applies to himself in spite of failing to conform to them, it is inevitable that he will feel some ambivalence about his own self" (1963: 106). This identity ambivalence within our very own self-understanding is a general condition affecting moderns. We earlier saw a specific instance when we looked at the identity ambivalence felt by modern Orthodox Jews.

In a suggestive comparison, Takeo Doi (1986) builds on the duality of two Japanese concepts that grasp a family of opposing notions such as mind/face, private/public, back/front. This cultural dichotomy of experience generates its own kind of ambivalence and functions analogously to soul/body or subject/object in Western culture. Given that there is an American ideal-typical image that combines culturally valued personal characteristics: for example, young, male, rich, well-schooled, athletic, smart, successful, handsome, healthy, straight-toothed, etc., it becomes obvious that few persons fulfil that ideal. Besides, even those who approximate it eventually realize that ideal features are held only for a limited and precarious time. Think of youth or health. Like the cultural ideal of being the "fastest gun" in the West, life, if not another gun, robs everyone of ideal attributes. In a word, cultural hero systems render each person more or less stigmatized in the powerful sense of being a self who possesses an attribute that carries a negative stereotypical meaning. Everyone is somewhere, somehow stigmatized, and thus potentially aware of identity ambivalence and self-alienation. Of course, as soon as we act contrary to our moral ideals, ambivalence is apt to become guilt. Ernest Becker (1975) argues that the dualism of the person, captured in his definition of humans as "gods with anuses," puts the worm of ambivalence in the core of character.

*Looking at Intimacy*

A critical perspective on contemporary contradictions highlights their effects on the quest for intimacy. Wexler (1983: 151–56) argues that socio-cultural contradictions effect private ambivalence. Ambivalent persons have two interpretative paths for making sense of experience. Either they seek respite within private worlds by attributing reasons for ambivalence to themselves; they subjectivize ambivalence. Or they recognize socio-cultural contradictions generating ambivalence and react against them; they "socialize" their mixed emotions. Popular, therapeutic, or individualistic solutions to intimacy are vacuous or harmful if they fail to link the problem with socio-cultural conditions.

The emptiness, lack of commitment, and narcissistic self-seeking that often mark the excessive quest for success are derivations from ideologies of atomistic individualism, utilitarianism, and profit maximization. These ideologies colonize consciousness with such existential force that intimacy is transformed into another individualistic exchange relationship captured in the phrases: What's in it for me? Is she (or he) the best I can get? I've reached the point of diminishing returns with him (her). Such translations of intimacy corrode collective goals that define solidary relationships. There is no cash equivalent for love. Ideological contradictions add to painful ambivalence even within the sacred bonds of intimacy.

If socio-cultural contradictions are plausibly linked to intimate relationships, there may be parallel links with collective movements. We can extend Marris' argument about the "impulse" of conservatism as humans try to retain predictability and control over their lives in the face of ineluctable change. As in bereavement, he argues that the struggle for meaning in the face of change, growth, and loss is a universal source of ambivalence as family and friends die or tribal identities and warm neighborhoods are destroyed. Ambivalence, like death, needs to be ritually enacted and defined, lest it fuel extreme responses in collective or individual action.

## Selected Hypotheses Underwriting The Story

Much of this story is speculative. It is derived from bits of theoretical reflection and occasional empirical references that illustrate a specific part of what we may call the ambivalence hypothesis. This section presents selected statements that hopefully have sufficient force to make the story plausible and fruitful. I recognize and indeed invite alternative hypotheses to support the stories that must be told about the modern condition.

The first assumption concerns an implied comparison between modern and other types of societies. Without a rigorous typology, I still use an implied comparison between modern and, let us say, traditional society, either in the sense of an earlier period of our society or in the sense of a comparison with contemporary societies thought to be "less modern." Obviously, it is a formidable task to document systematic comparison among societies, a task not undertaken here. Nevertheless, there are differences that are worth positing to help understand the modern condition, while we remain aware of the undemonstrated quality of the underlying comparisons.

At any rate, the first hypothesis is the following:

Hypothesis 1: *As societies become more modern, social psychological pluralism increases.*

Modern societies are taken to be more pluralistic than traditional societies; so too, therefore, is modern consciousness. This proposition is standard fare for social analysts, but it is difficult to demonstrate. The general understanding looks to such developments as the knowledge and population explosions; differentiation and specification in social institutions; the shrinking of the world through transportation and communication such that different ways of living, thinking, and feeling collide as they become available to more, shall we say, "earthlings"; and simply, the increasing rate of change fueled by mobility, markets, knowledge, and technology. With knowledge and action augmented by more powerful technological instruments like nuclear power, comes an increased scope of responsibility over wider territorial expanse and longer future implications. The age-old act of cutting firewood now creates deserts; clearing jungle forests for cattle grazing lessens available oxygen for the foreseeable future; nuclear accidents render areas uninhabitable beyond the species' time frame; and a nuclear holocaust may end mammalian life-support systems. The pluralism of modern society enters personal payoff schemas for knowledge, feelings, decision-making, and action.

The telling implication in this theme is that institutional and cognitive pluralism is linked to the structure of defined feelings. This leads to the second hypothesis.

Hypothesis 2: *As social psychological pluralism increases, ambivalence increases.*

This hypothesis follows from the first through the simple, but here undemonstrated, assumption that the internalized structures of institutional arrangements, knowledge, and decision-making are related to the structures of feelings and emotions. If Peter Berger (1980) is correct that to be modern is to be heretical, that is, forced to choose among conventional ways of acting or even between conventional ways and new alternatives, then moderns are likely to feel emotionally drawn to two or more of the options. Given the pluralism of the modern context, and assuming that each option for action has emotional weight, the modern person *feels* drawn in more than one direction.

The alternative would be to suppose that one course of action has only positive emotional weight attached to it and the others are neutral or negative. In the complexity of the modern context, such emotional "univalence" is unlikely; we need only check our own experience, others' accounts, or policy debates on major issues. The implication of Hypothesis 2 is that institutional arrangements of modern society expose members to more ambivalence-inducing situations than more traditional societies. A second implication is that the increased scope of responsibility and increasingly powerful technological intervention extend the outcomes of future action that moderns can imagine and feel. The complexity and crowding, as it were, of modern emotional life increase the probability that contradictory feelings or mixed emotions are experienced.

Hypothesis 3: *As societies become more modern, they have fewer "transcendental attitudes."*

The sources of ambivalence are empirical and objective social events, objects, and structures. A modern who feels ambivalent is likely in contact with and responding to real events. Modern pluralism would generate ambivalence in anyone who responded with feeling to the events that make up the reported state of the world. Today, in other words, it is not ambivalence that has to be explained, but its absence; not the ambivalent person, but the person who experiences singly defined feelings.

It is the empirical plausibility of ambivalent feelings that is addressed by the term, "transcendental attitudes." I do not intend to wax, or more likely, wane philosophical by using the word "transcendental." It has one guiding purpose here. If there is any appeal in the ideas of contradictory cognitive, decisional, or emotional experiences such that moderns find themselves abulic, i.e., unable to act decisively because they are drawn in two directions at once, and if, nevertheless, moderns do act, and often with no experience of contradictory emotions, then there are attitudes that combine contradictory elements to allow decisive action. It is such synthesizing attitudes I refer to by the term, transcendental, that is, able to combine contradictory components into a sufficient unity to allow decision and action.

Where are transcendental possibilities? Some symbols combine opposites into unities. *Reconciliatio oppositorum,* the synthesis of opposites, is what symbols can do. They are free of the logical, empirical, and discursive restraints on positivist thought. Nor are they bound by time, space, or narrow rules of rationality. This synthetic function of symbols has long been located in the domains of religion and the arts, or in general, within the semantic order of mythopoeic thought.

Some may argue that there is an underlying unity to all symbol systems, including science, engineering, or interpretation, as well as art and religion. I assume a difference between the last two and those symbolic orders with systematic empirical referents, culturally defined causes, or institutional research branches that deal with natural forces from the smallest molecule to the largest order of cosmic events. These are the physical, behavioral, and social sciences, and history.

Disciplined though mythopoeic inquiries are taken as dealing with constructions beyond the reach of systematic and public empirical evidence; nor are they associated with institutionalized research branches nor culturally recognized forms of causality. Simply, although individual leaders consult the stars, no nation-states are totally organized according to mythopoeic thought. The resurgence of Fundamentalism in major religious traditions is a partial exception, but even in societies in which a Fundamentalist form of religion takes power, it relies on the material technologies and empirically based rationalities of modern warfare, oil and energy production, knowledge dissemination, market arrangements, and industry in the service of its ideology.

The hypothesis leads us to expect more unresolved ambivalence in modern societies than would have been the case in traditional societies. In the latter, the symbolic realism of religion and art were more integrated into the social and political order. As a result, members of those societies would have cognitive and social resources for reconciling contradictory feelings. Mythic beings are half beast and half human. Angels and spirits inhabit another world as well as our own bodies. Traditional Western humans are bodies and souls or minds or psyches. Spiritual or quasi-spiritual beings are invoked to explain real events. As in Medieval times, the world may be transformed from objective events occurring at arm's length or at one's fingertips, to battles between real beings known within one's experience rather than before one's eyes or in one's hands. God and the Devil fought for control of the world within consciousness and consciences—the cognate terms suggests that there was hardly any distinction between what one knew about the world and the moral arena in which one experienced good and bad forces.

A world transformed into a battleground of personal

beings representing good and evil would leave the Medieval tensed ambivalently. Experiencing a simultaneous pull in opposite directions, to do good and to commit sin, the Medieval would not define the experience as ambivalence, but as the Devil against God's grace, each a real force within the person but not issuing from the person's subjectivity. The secular consciousness, and it is fair to say, secularized conscience, of the modern would attribute that experience to the interaction of empirical "things" outside of experience and the existential attitude of the person, but not to real spiritual beings that act within the individual. The Medieval construction is reversed by modern imaginings in which the person is transformed into a "being" within the reality of a computer program and display screen. In the Medieval world, the transcendent being, God or the Devil, comes to abide within the inner world of the person. In the modern world, transcendence for some is represented by the computer that gives reality to the person who goes to dwell in it (cf. Turkle 1984).

Strong enclaves or movements of traditional types of religion remain within the modern world. In the previous chapter, for example, certain kinds of Fundamentalist worldviews, especially concerning eschatology or End Time thinking, are interpreted as a response to ambivalence toward nuclear weapons. The ambivalence-resolution hypothesis does not argue that Fundamentalist believers accept future events like Rapture, Armageddon, or the saving return of Jesus with the explicit intention of resolving ambivalence. Such an intentional and behavioral translation would not be true to a sociological perspective: consequences that have observable and patterned outcomes, even beneficial ones, do not have to be intended in order to be analytically relevant. Such intentional reductionism reflects an exaggerated individualistic worldview. To be sure, we often claim that we act for certain reasons that may be true enough, but, even if true, they are hardly the whole story.

In his analysis of the "restructuring" of American religion from differences based on denomination to divisions based on conservative versus liberal ideology, Robert

Wuthnow (1988a) finds ambivalence a useful idea, though he does not use the term in a systematic way. In passages concerned with culture, the symbolic-expressive aspects of social behavior, Wuthnow sees an American religion ambivalent to its own past and the nation's future (31, 46), and an ambivalent American state wrestling with the dual responsibilities of building particularistic national identity and of working for the global good (255). A remarkable though unintegrated chain of passages offers a schematic social psychological theory of the ambivalence of American society toward what he pinpoints as its dominant motif: technology-driven capitalism. Wuthnow states that American religion is ambivalent toward mere self-interest (276) and materialism (265). Furthermore, there is deep ambivalence toward the seemingly unstoppable power of technology that Americans "love and hate" with "adulation and fear." There is a danger that the "critical balance" may break apart, however, and technology will fuel a self-legitimating myth of unbridled capitalism and consumption (295). In the final view, American religion's emphasis on "stewardship, equality, peace, love, and ultimate worth" implants ambivalence in the heart of inner-worldly motivation for, and interpretation of capitalism, the motor of modern society (249, 321). In this, conservative and liberal religionists can agree.

Analogous to these differences in religious worldviews, the form and function of art now reenforce similar conclusions. Traditionally, we see art magnifying human characteristics in scale and direction beyond the reach of puny individuals. Huge pyramids, lofty towers, giant colossus, magnificent tiered gardens, sweeping and spired buildings for worship and rule—these were some of the architectural achievements of ancient societies. The analogy between religion and art is seen in the uplifting grandeur of Medieval gothic cathedrals, uniting fact and yearning into stone stories telling of ascent from the vale of tears to the heaven of happiness.

Similarly, verbal arts told stories that had a dramatic structure of linear narrative with, as Aristotle ingenuously states, a beginning, middle, and end. Contrast such simple dramatic structure with that of montages, potpourris, or dance videos characteristic of modernist media. With their simple structure, traditional verbal arts presented paragons of action, virtue, comedy, and tragedy whose stories offered vicarious experiences in which opposites could be reconciled. Love and duty, incest and order, fear and pity, freedom and law, conscience and convention—the perennial oppositions that make up our feeling, knowing, and moral lives were combined in the dramatic action and resolved in the denouement of epochal stories and mythic achievements.

Oedipus, Antigone, Dionysius, Caesar, and the populist Everyman, Utopians, and that tragic long-face hero, Don Quixote, lived dramatic lives in which the opposites of their times were brought to tragic resolution, typically, as Aristotle noted, in death. Death, however, was not a meaningless end of life, a mere cessation of breathing and behavior. Rather, within the transcendental framework informing a traditional moral outlook, death takes on meaning as symbolizing the individual's participation in a moral order that is greater and more real than heaving, pulsing organic life. In identifying with the tragic hero or heroine, Everyperson can invest, forge, cleanse personal feelings of intense contradictions. In so doing, the group gives life to the person. The person lives, not as an individual atomistically struggling to find meaning for one's life, but as a participant in the larger life of that mythic hero. The tragic mask is a form of collective life that gives meaning to the heaving body behind it as well as to those tensed before it in the amphitheater.

We arrive at another view of the leitmotif: modern society is characterized by an ambivalence that did not socioculturally "exist" in traditional societies. This statement is offered in the mode of an hypothesis rather than a demonstrated historical conclusion. This is an essay toward an interpretive angle on contemporary society, not a treatise on comparative historical analysis. In addition, the ambivalence hypothesis needs careful understanding. A variety of corollaries are wrapped into that single proposition: moderns confront contradictory emotions more frequently than members of simpler societies; moderns lack synthesizing mythopoeic transcendental stories for reconciling their contradictory emotions; and finally, conflicting emotions have become a recognized social object with the currency of a specific word and concept to realize the experience. Once a complex of feelings is responded to as a social object, it becomes an institutionalized reality that persons can recognize, interpret, and integrate into their lives. An overarching theme in this discussion is that modern culture has constructed ambivalence as a social object. Ambivalence is part of our age's self-understanding. Yet, modern society is less able to resolve that anxiety-inducing condition it evokes within our experience.

### On The One Hand... But On The Other...!

Why should mixed emotions, even contradictory ones, be such a problem? After all, humans have two hands and two feet that could be seen as opposites, and they not only get along, they offer us a far better grasp than one "synthesized" hand or foot could do! If only emotions worked like opposing hands or thumbs. But perhaps there is an underlying wisdom in the analogy: one response to ambivalence is simply to live with the mixed emotions. Rather than experience the mixing as pain and anxiety to be resolved or avoided, the latter-day stoic can simply grit one's teeth and take the ambivalence cold turkey, as it were. The mixed experience can be a sign and cost of modernity; the push and pull of contradictory emotions may be symbolically transformed from vacillating weakness to precious sensitivity to the play of modern forces. Ambivalence may be redefined as a modern virtue. Books could be written and courses taught about the new-found paragon, the heroic ambivalent. Therapeutic groups could organize to help impoverished "univalents" who are traumatically blocked from feeling proper ambivalence toward family, job, society, or environment!

Such handy redefinition could be part of an informed worldview. Just as an informed citizen should know more than one side of crucial issues, so too ought that citizen feel what persons on different sides of the issue experience. The Devil can quote scripture and remain evil. What if the Devil also felt what God's love is like—could the Devil still be the source of evil? Not likely. Feeling what others feel and not merely knowing what they know is a preferred interpretive stance, and one which the modern world makes all the more imperative given the depth of its crises.

If we shift focus from the inner world to the demand for collective and institutional life, the glow of ambivalence takes an ominous hue. The striking paradox of action is that as organisms and collective extensions of organisms, we are condemned, not so much to be free, but to be determined to suffer or enjoy the outcomes of whatever course of action we follow, regardless of how free we feel. The inevitability of outcomes once we start acting makes the ambivalence of the leader or policy maker utterly contradictory: there is a necessity to go on acting built into the very nature of an ongoing act, even if we really do not know what to do or what will come next!

The pilot of our 747 cannot enjoy ambivalence as a signal of modernity as she faces a split-second decision whether to bank left or ascend right: evasive action must be taken or the oncoming Airbus and our 747 will crash midair. When action is imperative, ambivalence be damned! Somehow, moderns must overcome a characteristic of their era and act competently. In a split-second crisis, training may do the trick. In societal or biographical crises slow to take shape and painfully complex to see through, however, the worm of ambivalence may gnaw more slowly. It cannot be eradicated completely.

### Addenda Toward an Ambivalent Agenda

Moderns are condemned, not so much to be free, as to be ambivalent. The hero system needs to face up to the great reversal; Charlie Brown, who has a hard time deciding what to do, is the archetypal cultural hero. Rambo is an ephemeral exaggeration, as is Luke Skywalker or George Washington

Hayduke. We have met the enemy, and they is us—the gram-
matical errors are necessary to convey the idea. Contrary to
cultural norms, to *feel* ambivalence, to *be* ambivalent is not
to be inadequate, unformed, or immature. Hardly! Ambivalence is a sign of modernity, though to be sure, it is a sign that
must be contradicted and its sources absorbed into larger
meaning, emotional as well as cognitive.

In recent decades, social psychologists have generated
three trends of reflection relevant here. All three contradict
and correct folk understandings about how or why Americans act. I refer to the "cognitive dissonance" construct;
studies of obedience to immoral authority; and the contradiction between the helping hand and the fear of involvement felt by those who witnessed the murder of Kitty Genovese, and whose darkened windows set off research into
the dynamics of "bystander ethics." These vectors of reflection are based on models of cognitive or attitudinal consistency derived from the principle that humans are rather
rational actors who strive for consistency among personal
judgments and attitudes, especially those concerning self-
understanding.

Cognitive consistency models threw powerful if partial
light on human behavior. More to our point, however, they
enabled researchers to challenge stereotypes and common
sense judgments such as: persons evaluate the positive
worth of an activity by the material profit they get from it;
American democracy forms citizens who are morally autonomous, believe in fair play, and would not violate their conscience to inflict pain on innocent victims; and finally, Americans go to the aid of those less fortunate than themselves,
especially those in desperate need, such as a screaming
woman about to the murdered. Research shows the opposite
of these stereotypes to be perhaps the weightier truth.

Leon Festinger (1957) illustrated, for example, that persons who receive low material reward for putting up with an
annoying and boring job thought better of the job than did
those who were better paid. Payment seemed to free up realistic evaluation of participation. Paid subjects recounted an
experience as it is: boring and annoying. Money is not the

only, and perhaps not even the most important, source of value for judging the worth of what we do. Apparently, there is a dynamic of consistency and significance in the way we think about what we do, how we feel, and who we are that is more fundamental than the extrinsic attachment of monetary sums to our behavior or our person. Of course, money has its power, and attitudinal, behavioral, or self-consistency is not the only motive at work. The juggernaut of material symbolism may continue to dominate self-understanding ever more and more, even as it transforms our ability to absorb experiences in and for themselves.

In his studies that spawned probing questions, Stanley Milgram tackled a major issue and a central cultural myth: the autonomous American unmoved by social forces is put into a situation that induces many, and occasionally all, participants to act against conscience and inflict wrongful pain over the protests and screams of the innocent "victim." Psychological thinkers and lay judges grossly underestimated the frequency and depth of Americans' docile acquiescence to actions recognized as contrary to our ethos of fairness, autonomy, and moral responsibility. Americans from varied walks of life yielded to apparent scientific authority and obeyed orders that contradicted their consciences. The contradiction was evidenced by anguished squirming, verbal exclamations, and post-experiment questionnaire or interview data. Milgram notes that, "there were both obedient and defiant outcomes, frequently accompanied by extreme tension" (1975: 42).

A similar conflict of conscience and social pressure is evident in the Kitty Genovese case. A young woman was pursued by an attacker, wounded, pursued further, and eventually killed while many city residents heard, were moved by, and ignored her cries for help. This became one of those rare events that provided a paradigm for experimental social psychologists, in this case to study "bystander effects": behavior, attitudes, and motivation to attend, intervene, or disattend the scene. Americans were shocked by the case. Like the cognitive dissonance and authority-obedience findings, the Kitty Genovese incident sent a message about identity, motivation, and values that Americans did not want to hear.

As scholars who study the attribution of explanations and motives tell us, we tend to interpret events so that our self-worth and esteemed identity survive intact. If Americans did not come to the aid of a woman about to be murdered, or even lift up the phone to call the police, then the explanation cannot be that Americans are uncaring or immoral. Rather, there must be some social psychological force at work that blunts or deflects our native goodness. Apparently, the mere presence of unknown others inhibits everyone's helping response (Latané and Darley 1970). Both attributions may have validity; the challenging issue is how much and in what way do individual and social structural factors come into play in shaping our perceptions and responses. Bystander research tries to gauge these questions, but the overall issue remains: there is conflict between beliefs and values the individual brings to the scene and the situational forces shaping individual responses. City dwellers saw ambivalence, as well as the killer, stalking Kitty Genovese.

Standard interpretations of these paradigmatic studies emphasize the cognitive resolution of inconsistencies. Without denying this cognitive emphasis, there is another angle. Of course, individuals in these situations experience tension, as Milgram notes. Why? Because they experience the conflict of dual values, expectations, commands: obey scientific authority vs. do what you believe is right. The tension manifests not only cognitive conflict, but a deeper experience of emotional ambivalence. Humans are sentient actors motivated by the totality of demand characteristics of self in the situation. Adequate interpretations include the simultaneous push-pull of contradictory emotions that generates the tension rationalized into two choices each with its attendant costs/benefits calculated in a rational preference for this goal as more valued, and this means as more efficient. Part of the scene is an emotional calculus to escape the dis-ease or tension. "Be still, my heart," is a cry answered by action often pursued precisely because of the cries of that heart, not the calculations of the mind.

Milgram (1975) provides evidence of mixed emotions. A panoply of dramaturgical indicators were present: body language like squirming, sweating, leaping from one's seat, and stalking out of the room; verbal indicators such as blurting out, asides addressed to no one, talking to one's self or oneself, and a variety of exclamations; and post-experiment debriefings by questionnaires, interviews, and group discussions. A similar structure of experience faces bystanders and witnesses of crimes that violate their sense of fair play: they are both drawn to help out, and repulsed by fear.

These research trends fit the model presented earlier as analogs of Merton's "core" sociological ambivalence: contradictory expectations associated with a single role, status, or situation. It is important that the construct, "expectations," include the totality of dispositions readying the organism for action, and not merely an abstracted cognitive dimension. These research traditions both document secondary ambivalence generated by contradictory imperatives of modern culture, and illustrate the predominance of cognitive models among social psychologists as they reflect that culture back to us.

In a word, the success and power of these research traditions provide cases in point of the paradoxical effect of modern culture. They both provide codes of conduct that are overly cognitive and elicit emotional responses that are mixed and often contradictory. Moderns act to resolve emotional dis-ease and allay ambivalence even as they claim that they are acting for cognitive, indeed rational, reasons—an available and acceptable account. As a result, we learn to "flatten" our experience, to compress its total flow into abstracted categories that presumably guide decisions and actions. Our experiential world is made into an overly cognitive "Flatland" (Abbott 1983).

## To Be or Not To Be

The question for Flatlanders is "to be or not to be." For the first time in history, this question is posed with the

means at hand for ending species being for the higher mammals. Ambivalence is not merely a challenge of interpersonal relations, individual consistency, or institutional dilemmas; it is at hand in the core of action. Humans must learn
to live with ambivalence or it may drive them to the final
paradox of self-destruction.

What options face a realistically ambivalent Flatlander?
A modern can suffer ambivalence passively and simply follow routines that ease tension momentarily. Paraphrasing C.
Wright Mills' characterization of self-defined middle class
moderns, this is acquiescence as a "cheerless robot," an
instance of the mindless mass canonized by Dostoevsky in
the Grand Inquisitor scene. A second option is to act decisively in spite of ambivalence, a kind of stoic solution. As
basketball cant would have it, the modern stoic scores
"right in the face" of ambivalence. Stoic realism is possible
for the disciplined few, but it is not likely to generate a collective solution nor provide institutional correctives to the
sources of ambivalence. Besides, it hurts to be a stoic, even
if one maintains mental discipline and symbolically transforms hunger into an irrelevant condition because it is
beyond the control of one's will. The stoic solution flies in
the face of the modern search for pleasure and security.

Flatlanders have two other options: overcome ambivalence with new or recycled mythopoeic constructions such
as primitive, encysted, sectarian, or exotic religions; or,
more modernly, "numb" their sensitivities by ignoring
ambivalence-inducing issues, deflecting contradictory feelings, or invalidating one of them by overly embracing the
other and transforming it into a total experience. Robert J.
Lifton developed the idea of "psychic numbing" in his
attempt to understand moderns' psychological coping with
the riveting ambivalence of the Bomb (see Lifton and Falk
1982). He noted also a process of "doubling" by persons
who live contradictions. One twin self is real in each contradictory domain, and the twins do not always talk to each
other. We could generalize Lifton's construct into the idea of
a cultural "analgesic," that is, rituals and myths that double
us numb like cultural pain killers. Analgesics are delivered

by encysted or sectarian groups, or carried by central myths. Modernity offers other coping devices revolving around material "trippers" (cf. Weigert and Sughrue 1988), like hi-tech gadgets, drugs, alcohol, media addictions, or salvation by power or profit. The modern quest is to "pay no heed," "feel no pain," or be numbed or doubled in collective crises. Analgesics deaden ambivalence, thus warding off abulia and agonia.

A cultural pathos of modernity is that its characteristic features, such as science, technology, computer rationality, near instantaneous communication, bio- and material engineering, indeed, any form of functional rationality *cannot* resolve ambivalence. These forms of rationality *generate* further ambivalence by enlarging the scope of responsibility; entailing more and longer lasting consequences, both foreseen and unforeseen; and providing no intrinsic values to guide action. In a word, the characteristic institutions of modern society are the driving forces of an ambivalence-inducing culture. Alas! This statement is the larger message, and it deserves serious study.

A powerful option, but one with a high price, is to revert to traditional ambivalence-resolving identities: religious, ideological, nationalistic, aesthetic, scientistic—in perhaps decreasing order of liklihood. As we saw, some traditional religious resolutions involve belief in trans-empirical categories like literal interpretation of the Bible or predictive prophecy, and expected empirical events like Rapture, Jesus's Second Coming, and Armageddon. Traditional religious resolutions include a role for Satan or mythically enlarged enemies, such as the part assigned to the Soviet Union, China, or an emerging European Anti-Christ in the worldview of American Fundamentalists, and in an ironical mirror image, to the United States in the eyes of Iranian Fundamentalists. Who is God's sword or arch enemy depends on where one is born.

Part of the cost of traditional resolutions derives from the collective nature of mythopoeic realities. Cosmic myths and transcendent worldviews cannot be created, rendered plausible and transmitted across generations by individuals

qua individuals. This is the social realism axiom: only collective life supplies and renders plausible symbols through
which individuals can transcend individuality. Moderns
who embrace a traditionalist resolution of ambivalence
must join a group, either physically, cognitively, or emotionally, that provides rituals, ideologies, and a dramaturgical
infrastructure for socially constructing that resolution.
Such is one interpretive angle on the rise and strength of
reactionary and Fundamentalist movements around the
world. The proof lies in the consoling power of their socially
constructed divine world (cf. Ammerman 1987).

On the other hand, individuals act modernly by pursuing self-interests in acquisitive or expressive individualism
(cf. Bellah et al. 1985). Self-interests, however, are inherent-
ly short term. Self-time is foreshortened time. Action guid-
ed by a narrow, this-worldly interpretation of "What's in it
for me?" cannot guide decisions in long-term environmental, civic, or biographical terms. Those who wish to be
thoroughly modern must embrace, most likely with exaggerated tension, one of the mixed emotions. They can pursue pleasure, success, money, thrills, or whatever is at
hand. The key is that meaning is sought in action, not in
being, community, or a transcendent category. Moderns
are taught to be short-term rational actors. Yet, as Max
Weber rightly intoned, short-term rationality leads to long-
term irrationality. The shout that God, and any traditional
configuration, is dead in whatever realm: art, natural language, philosophical experience, folk wisdom, status symbols, or rites of passage, echos through the search for
meaning in a disenchanted world.

The modern dilemma, seen from the perspective of
ambivalence, takes this form: socio-cultural dynamics generate mixed emotions in meaning and action and provide
shifting, short-term schemas for resolving affective and
actional dilemmas. Shifting, short-term schemas are
ephemeral resolutions of symptoms, not of causes. As a
result, moderns are faced with mixed emotions and ineffectual resolutions, and left with deeper ambivalence: whether
to continue searching for short-term resolutions or opt for a

powerful, long-term symbolic synthesis of opposition, that is, a return to traditional community structures and content, or religious plausibility structures that render traditional forms operationally credible (cf. MacIntyre 1984).

The final strategy is the most unmodern move a modern could make into encysted traditionalism—the reverse of simple-minded evolutionary models of social life. This unmodern move reopens the human nature issue: clearly, moderns experience selves as something more than a "nothing but" product of the society and times that produce them. Whether an anthropological conservative instinct for dimly remembered ways of life (cf. Marris 1975); a Piercean intelligent instinct for meaning in life (cf. Rochberg-Halton 1986); an organically ordered need for cognitive or emotional closure; or a remedy for pierced personalities and cracked characters, some moderns experience powerful religious motivation.

The master religious inquiry, Am I among the Saved? that has broken cultures apart and driven men and women to throw themselves into the flames or to journey below the horizon piques us still. Contrary to optimistic functionalist reasoning, traditional solutions for mixed emotions, the *reconciliatio oppositorum,* is a trans-empirical plausibility upheld by social power, not by the exigencies of natural imperatives. Scholars who read the social evolutionary record find ambivalence-resolving symbolic systems that have succeeded, at least long enough to leave their mark. Failed solutions leave a fainter trail. Furthermore, scholars suffer the self-projection fallacy of believing that what produced our species so far has clearly worked, and thus it is in tune with the underlying forces of nature, the overarching powers of supernature, or the hybristic dynamics of history or any "isms" that can conquer the environment and render it a means of aggrandizement.

The empirical possibilities, however, are more complex and ominous: even symbol systems functional till today need not be viable for tomorrow. Symbol systems do not spring only from the imperatives of life; they can be profoundly anti-life and species destructive, just as genetic and

phenotypical adaptations ticketed some species for extinction. DNA and radiation research may keep lettuce from
spoiling, and yet, in staying the rot, help set the stage for
humans' final act. Optimistic sociobiological and social evolutionary writers may pass off a notion of "co-evolution"
that implies complementary laws of nature and culture
guaranteeing a sufficient probability of reproducing germ
plasm to better adapted generations. Some kind of co-evolution may be a norm and value, but it is hardly an empirical
certainty. Evolution is toward species extinction to make
room for better adapted species. Humans are *within* natural
evolution, not outside it in some asymptotic co-evolution.
Abstracted structuralists may posit symbol systems that
work with no link to the material chances of species survival. The point is that all symbol systems, to the extent
that they are effective, that is, guide and motivate action,
have physical consequences on the probabilities of survival. And by their fruits Ye shall know them.

The autonomy of symbol systems as motivational constructs makes room for a model of culture *versus* nature.
Indeed, that conflict characterizes modernity. For the first
time, humans are engaged in critical interventions at the
core of life-support systems that are materially finite, even
though the needs and ideologies that legitimate intervention are symbolically infinite. Solutions to ambivalence are
symbolic constructions. The autonomy and unbounded-
ness of symbolic systems, added to psychological over-
reactance as persons embrace one pole in the ambivalent
situation, suggest the caution, criticism, and perhaps fear
with which contemporary resolutions are to be weighed.

This may sound like a paradoxical turn to take at this
point. I have argued that ambivalence is perhaps basic to
the human condition and empirically generated by contemporary structures, and that it is anxiety inducing and
painful. Now I am arguing that resolutions may be dangerous and fearful because ambivalence leads to over-reaction;
elicits symbolic resolutions that may be autonomous from
and possibly in conflict with life-support systems; and may
generate a worldview and motivate action that are anti-life.

This Catch 22 dilemma is illustrated by the case we discussed above: Fundamentalist apocalypticism contains a symbolic system that motivates believers to accept if not welcome the likelihood of nuclear devastation as a prophesied step toward Christ's Kingdom on a cleansed earth.

These unmodern moderns apply a traditional symbol system to a contemporary frightful situation. Such applications are risky. They resolve ambivalence, but they carry motives for courses of action that lead to solutions worse than the cure. Fundamentalist End Time thinking is a larger and extensive manifestation of this paradox, and it may be found in apocalyptic eschatologies around the world, from the United States to Iran. Secular ideologies of nations on opposite sides can call for reasonable, life-supporting self-interest: the U.S.S.R., the Peoples Republic of China, and the U.S.A. can make deals that are based on empirically available processes and probable outcomes, and not on prophesied events beyond empirical verification. Just as the Soviet Union and the United States seek mutual verification in nuclear arms negotiations, so too, moderns must rely on empirical verification in their End Time thinking. Imagine a scientific, materialistic, atheistic Communist having an ideology that would welcome the nuclear holocaust! If a person interprets the world through a perspective limited to empirical science, restricted to only material reality, and with no belief in a transcendent Being, then he or she would fear the destruction of the life-support systems. The earth we all walk on is all that person believes in. There is no Millennium to follow Armageddon. A burnt-over earth remains just that. Which finger, poised over the Nuclear Button, would you think more likely to push It: one inspired by a transcendent eschatology prophesying Christ's Second Coming; or one innervated by scientific materialism predicting an unlivable earth?

Some unmodern moderns, even though they are of us, are indeed risky. The probability that Fundamentalist traditionalists would make the risky shift to a transcendent, supernatural framework for acting in the mundane world defines the likelihood that they would be willing to use

empirical nuclear bombs to bring about their transcendentally framed world. Clearly, traditional resolutions to
ambivalence may carry risks that are too costly.

An alternative suggests itself. The functional unity of
worldviews such as religion comes in part from their mythic, cosmic closure. They offer the security and certainty of a
common known beginning and a shared meaningful end.
From the shared sense of a common origin and common
fate, humans build communities with a shared identity and
common course of action. Those shared value configurations need to confront modern crises of environment, societal relations, and self-understanding. Perhaps humans
need a revivified mythopoeic story of human origins in the
primordial molecular soup of the universe and of the too
proximate possibility of a human end in nuclear or environmental disaster. The awe of transcendence will ever render
such an account yet another source of ambivalence, but
perhaps an ambivalence stood on its head and to be
enjoyed as we design common courses of survival with
those who are most unlike us in other ways. Above all, if we
can be ambivalent to our own selves, we can not be certain
toward anyone.

## Materialists or Postmaterialists?

There are survey indications of a two-fold polarization
of modern culture. Wuthnow's studies of contemporary
American religion find traditional identifiers such as religious denomination crossed by conservative versus liberal
value configurations. In some ways, conservative Catholics
are more like conservative Baptists than either group is like
liberal members of its own denomination. To predict attitudes toward nuclear issues, environment, feminism, sexual
morality, abortion, or welfare spending, accuracy appears
to increase with knowledge of the conservative-liberal axis
rather than denominational affiliation. Wuthnow (1988a)
interprets this as a major cultural realignment within religious identities and collectivities. In advanced societies,

religion itself has become a rather free-floating cultural form applicable to varied and crisscrossing sets of issues (Beckford 1989).

In wide-ranging analyses of surveys from virtually all industrialized and European nations, Inglehart (1990) argues for a deep "cultural shift," confirming his earlier finding that modernity is characterized by what he calls a "postmaterialist" value configuration. Postmaterialist values center around a sustainable quality of life rather than continued economic growth, a position he labels "materialist." A sustainable quality of life correlates with opposition to nuclearism, big bureaucracy, and statism, and support of environmentism, civil and gender rights, and reasonable welfare provisions. He argues that the traditional left-right ideological axis based on acceptance or rejection of social change in the direction of greater inclusion and socio-economic equality is now crossed by an emerging materialism-postmaterialism axis based on priority given to economic growth for itself versus sustaining a certain quality of life. Conventional theory and predictions based on simple class ideology no longer grasp the cognitive or emotional situation of "First World" citizens. Scores on materialism-postmaterialism values are better predictors than single class indicators.

Inglehart finds that postmaterialist values are carried by the young, by the elite, and paradoxically for folk stereotypes, by the exemplar of contemporary consumerism, the Yuppie. Well off, professional, well educated, almost upper class Yuppies are the cultural carriers of postmaterialist values. There are strong generational differences that suggest such value configurations will grow wider and deeper in the future, at least in the First World with an already high level of consumption. Following a Maslowian model of hierarchy of values, those whose materialist needs are reasonably satisfied see the importance of growth for what? or institutions for whose good? questions, and move to recognize other's needs and the necessity of sustaining the natural environment. Almost paradoxically, postmaterialists are materially secure enough to be concerned with sustaining the very possibility of materialist well-being in nature and physical realities. It remains to be seen, however, whether the realism that Inglehart reads into postmaterialist values can counteract the unbridled romanticism of a modernity characterized by consumption for consumption's sake. Would postmaterialists, for example, restrain consumption and send the "abstinence dividend" to Brazil to underwrite preservation of Amazon rain forests?

Evidence for religious and cultural shifts in the United States and other First World nations suggests that their citizens feel the push-pull of crisscrossing cultural axes: denominational identity versus conservative-liberal ideology; left-right class-based ideology versus materialist-postmaterialist values. The modern form of emotional life is not felt by one's position on a simple we-they axis, but by pressures generated by vectors of crisscrossing cultural movements. Modernity is defined by a sense of crisis, an urgency that something must done. Yet, moderns are citizens who feel drawn in two or more directions at once. Ambivalence as an affective form of life does not allow action to proceed until it is numbed, resolved, or overridden. Although he does not use ambivalence as a technical term, Inglehart finds configurations of contradictory cultural values carried by elites sired by socioeconomic situations, historical events, and life course changes.

These cultural developments suggest macro-forces generating ambivalence with processes for controlling emotion akin to those delineated in Elias' "civilizing process" (1982, passim), and Slater's reading of group dynamics (1966). Slater explicitly pinpoints a moment in group dynamics at which the affective pressures toward both identifying with the group and separating from it threaten to tear a member in two. Slater recognizes the mixed feelings and, almost quaintly, goes to ethology for an interpretation. If a bird, for example, is torn equally between contradictory impulses toward fight or flight, it may resolve the mutually inhibiting impulses by a "displacement activity" that is unrelated but distracting, e.g., idle scratching or preening. Perhaps the combination of Inglehart's analysis and Slater's ethological aside delivers a more powerful lesson than either intended: is it possible that moderns, torn by ambivalence in critical situations, will resolve the mixed emotions by sitting around preening or idly scratching? Is this ethological displacement activity analogous to Lifton's numbing behavior that both brackets ambivalence and allays anxiety? One could hypothesize that analyses of media messages in Presidential discourse, religious homelitics, educational texts, and market-driven advertisements would document the scratch and preen interpretation of irrelevant conduct in ambivalent situations.

## Looking Janus in the Face(s)

The model underlying this essay is based on relationships across three levels of analysis: (1) sociocultural contradictions institutionalize (2) interpersonal contradictions that are (3) experienced as mixed emotions. The argument is open-ended and unprotected at each end. Within individual dynamics, for example, it is important to ask further whether there are sociobiological processes that generate contradictory sensations, conflicting behavioral impulses, and mixed feelings. This book has nothing to say about these questions. At the cultural end, there is an underlying assumption informing the essay, namely, a built-in dynamic of two contradictory processes that can in the abstract be thought of as culture and life. Following the leads of Georg Simmel and José Ortega y Gasset, human life is seen as a process that must be contained within the finite limit of form. Culture is form. Life, however, is forever breaking out of cultural forms. Cultural forms are constantly imposed, re-imposed, and at times, violently clamped upon life, both individual and collective, from prophetic condemnations to military massacres whether here or in Tiananmen Square. Modernity reflects Simmel's insistence on conflict and tragedy at the core of the human condition ontologically tensed between vital expansiveness and formal boundaries, and Ortega's smile at the irony of mass mentality that stupidly mistakes form for life or doltishly believes that life can be formless.

The dialectic of life and form shows various solutions. Such are the institutional arrangements that structure the human story. The guiding historical hypothesis of this essay is that modernity is characterized by the breakup of traditional solutions and their mix and match in the marketplace of ideas and ideologies. Suggestive operationalizatons of this mix and match are the contradictory tensions found in Western societies and, specifically, in the institutional dilemmas of the "first modern nation," the United States. As Alan Wolfe notes, "Given the paradoxes of modernity, there is little wrong . . . with being ambivalent—especially when there is so much to be ambivalent about" (1989: 211).

A strong metaphor of ambivalent selfhood is the "doubling" within the culture carrying identity of the professional who is co-opted into performing evil under the ideological illusion that it is good (Lifton 1986), or on a lesser note, into acting for personal profit rather than the good of the client or the commonweal, the predicament of the salaried professional. The modern self, as noted earlier, is stretched on the rack between impulse and institution (Turner 1976); between a gossamer illusory "inner self" and a less than legitimate and ultimately shallow "public self" (cf. Baumeister 1986). Though this racked tension is not a totally modern discovery, it has become a widely available cultural condition, whereas through history it appears to have been the hard-won insight of moral and aesthetic illuminati who broke the boundaries of their cultural forms.

There are widespread but uncodified appeals to ambivalence as an interpretive aid for making sense out of contemporary interpersonal relationships. A salient version of male-female relationships, for example, puts romantic love or lustful fun as the basis for intimacy and, in a paradox that the young often fail to see, for marriage. The cultural legerdemain says that romance is the basis for long-term, indeed, life-time commitment. This is a contradiction: romance is by definition transient, situational, and affective; lifetime commitment is permanent, institutional, and contractual. Institutionalized commitment cannot be grounded on impulsive affect. Is there any wonder that romantically attracted individuals about to enter matrimony feel profound ambivalence. Romance may be life, but marriage is form.

Nelson Foote saw ambivalence in the romantic love complex (1953). He went on to define authentic love as committed labor fruitful for the self-transcendence of the beloved, not as an ephemeral feeling. Yet, loveless labor is desiccated. Medievals taught that *laborare est orare,* linking work and prayer in their ultimate value narrative, and in modern times, Freud insisted that the dual wellsprings of a healthy life are work and love, *Arbeiten und Lieben.* Each vocabulary of value captures the basic tension, and agrees on the necessity of work, whatever their other differences. Love's labor must not be lost.

Underlying forms of perception are time and space. Ambivalence lies here as well. In time, we are born between the permanence perceived in the recurrent, periodic, and cyclic; and the change sensed in the individual, transient, and linear (Young 1988). In space, we are simultaneously here and there, or at least we can so see ourselves with a sense of space transformed into our place. Yi-Fu Tuan concludes his reflection on the evaluative experience of place, "topophilia," by noting that humans have ambivalent attitudes to wilderness, countryside, and city as both chaotic and orderly, clean and dirty, secure haven and dangerous site, and that there are historical reversals in such dual evaluations. The wilderness was long a place of danger, dirt, and disorder, but in modern times, it is a space of ecological safety, naturally non-polluted, and physically well-ordered (1974: 248). Such reflections suggest the larger set of contradictory categories underlying cultural forms that Mary Douglas (1970) codified with the analogous rubrics of dirty and clean that bespeak danger and purity.

The conflict between life and form is part of the socialization pattern that then defines a central developmental task for youth. Socialization means to inform young life with culture. A dominant instrument of modern culture is technology, a form that evokes ambivalent responses in the young. Kenneth Keniston (1968: 284) found rebellious youth of the Sixties both attracted to and repulsed by aspects of technology. They did not want to live with it, but they could not live practically without it. The half-buried car on "Earth Day" is an apt Janus symbol.

Of the many manifestations of technology, computer culture is a powerful form. In her study of "the second self" of young hackers, Sherry Turkle found recurrent strands of ambivalence toward both the embodied self and the circuited second self, the computer (1984: 197). Some hackers put the issue as a split between their depreciated "people selves" and their powerful "technology selves." Within MIT computer culture at the time, users are called "lusers" who log on with their "luser numbers" (199–200). At the same time, these computer lusers successfully exist in an artificial world in which they have a constructed identity that is in control. Older philosophers face the issue of artificial intelligence and computer "minds" as analogs of self. They raise anew the antinomies of emergence, unitary selfhood, or human ego. Ultimately, artificial intelligence runs up against the contradiction apparently at the heart of formal systems of thought: every formal system raises a question for which it cannot supply an answer. The center of mind, like the heart of the sacred, leaves humans tensed by ambivalence that secures them with closure and scares them with meaninglessness.

There are two strong if speculatively linked outcomes of ambivalence, one in the economic realm of consumer motivation and the other in the social psychology of professions in the service of ideologies. The former dynamic is carried by the middle class broadly conceived, and the latter by a class of professionals. Let us take the latter first.

In his literally painstaking study of Nazi and prisoner doctors operating the genocide of the concentration camps, Lifton (1986) uses the construct, "doubling" to understand how normal persons perpetuate systematic evil and continue functioning as professionals. His lengthy text is laced with analyses of protagonists' paradoxical situations, words, and actions. Furthermore, he finds severe ambivalence at critical points. I would hypothesize that the phenomenon of doubling is a universally available psychological dynamic in normalizing responses to ambivalence that is otherwise unbearable. In the genesis of pathological multiple personalities, Lifton states that we are likely to find serious "trauma, an atmosphere of extreme ambivalence, and severe conflict and confusion over identifications—all of which can also be instrumental in doubling" (422). The Nazi doctors double forth an "Auschwitz self" within whose social world the daily degradation, torture, and murder of thousands of victims not only is acceptable but is transformed into a preferred moral act. The Auschwitz self believes in such contradictory imperatives as "therapeutic killing" that is not in violation of, but demanded by, their identities as doctors. This imperative in macabre fashion evokes the paradox of detached concern at the ambivalent center of a doctor's imperative to act.

Lifton ends his treatise with reflections on the psychology of genocide, what I may call "speciescide," namely, actions that kill categories of humans or the entire species. He fears that the tendency toward doubling is built into the human species; made more likely by compartmentalized institutional arrangements characteristic of modern society; and rendered legitimate by totalizing ideologies that validate "our" worldview while nihilating "theirs." He suggests extending the analysis to other professionals besides doctors, e.g., technologists and scientists who devote their professional calling to build weapons capable of speciescide, i.e., nuclearism; psychiatrists who subordinate their medical ethos to help the state control its citizens; or bureaucrats who transform murderous actions into technical organizational problems, e.g., by referring to killing as "special treatment" and by devising more efficient and less costly treatments. In the end, Lifton believes that genocidal state regimes are characterized by "reactionary modernism" based on a "contradiction toward technology and modernism—not so much a contradiction as the most extreme ambivalence..." (494). He goes on to hope that professionals

can resist genocidal and murderous tendencies "by main-
taining a balance of what I call advocacy and detachment, of
clear ethical commitment and technical skill" (500). Buridan's ass has become Buridan's professional.

The tension of modern life is discernible in economic
motivation as well. Modern capitalist society, according to
Max Weber's thesis, was born ironically through the spiritual power of the Puritan, the ascetic this-worldly Protestant
ethical character. The Puritan was driven by religious anxiety about salvation made as real as the scene outside the
window by a literal eschatology of death and damnation.
The Puritan strove for salvation by following a calling
toward ceaseless economic activity whose fruits were not
profit or consumption, but material signs of God's predestination. Working out personal crisis through incessant economic activity fired the mighty engines of capitalist production. The historical irony is that a demanding religious
ethos helped give birth to an ethic of production that now
supplies its own motivation without, indeed often against,
any religious foundation. The theory by which the Puritan
interpreted economic success as a sure sign of predestined
salvation overcame the massively real tension felt between
being a citizen of a spiritual world and creature of a material
world. Puritan religiosity synthesized the felt tension into
motivation—the power to break with traditional ways of
thinking, feeling, and acting in daily life.

Colin Campbell follows Weber's lead and asks another
question: whence the power of that ethos so characteristic
today, an ethic of consumption? He complements Weber by
arguing that the same historical forces gave rise eventually
to a Romantic ethos of illusory, socially constructed pleasure as an emotional concomitant of consumption. Modern
society teaches us that it is good, indeed virtuous, to seek
emotional pleasure primarily by romantic consuming, not
through real bodily consuming. It is the illusion of pleasure,
the social emotion defined as pleasure, that is consumed.
Bodily pleasure is quickly sated and morally mixed. Illusory
pleasure is boundless and virtuous. To be a good modern,
one should consume. Campbell concludes by arguing that

"The cultural logic of modernity is not merely that of rationality; it is also that of passion. . . . Yet, more crucial than either is the tension generated between them . . . " (1987: 227). He sees this tension distributed over domains of knowledge occupations, between genders, and into stages of the lifecourse, with the Romantic ethos housed in the arts, helping professions, women, and youth. Nevertheless, every modern is motivated by both; their logical and moral contradictions are merged into the distinctive tensions of modern life. The middle-class individual is a "double"; there are "two beings inside him" (223).

## Summary

A guiding thesis of this essay is that traditional culture had forms to alleviate contradictory emotions. Primordial ambivalence is resolved through transcendental categories and collective rituals. Social structural ambivalence is overcome by institutional and interactional norms and feeling rules. The complementary thesis is that contemporary culture both creates ambivalence through contradictory cultural norms and structural imperatives, and has weak transcendental categories and rituals for alleviating it. We suggest interpreting today's world through the lens of ambivalence as a form of modern life.

Moderns face limited options to resolve ambivalence. First, they can go reactionary and resolve ambivalence through transcendental categories or a sectarian identity, or they can embrace one of the contradictory emotions. Second, they can institutionalize ambivalence by aligning behavioral norms and feeling rules so that part of the mixed emotions are acted out as in the careful touch of the concerned but detached doctor. Third, moderns can learn to act reasonably while experiencing unalleviated ambivalence, akin to Sartre's appeal to respond creatively to anxious moral dilemmas. The last solution leaves us with perhaps a new form of moral consciousness: acting decisively while experiencing contradictory emotions. Just as ambiguity and complexity eliminates the possibility of total objective certitude and moderns learn to act "rationally" with statistical "certitude" based on estimated probabilities of outcomes, so too ambivalent moderns eliminate total subjective or felt certitude as a criterion of moral action.

Modern culture generates deep ambivalences that need to be balanced, synthesized, or overcome. To be modern is to be a sundered and opposing self. A social scientific task is to trace the cultural and institutional lines of such opposition and the forces for generating and resolving them. The opposition can be read positively or negatively, as alienation or creative tension. Nevertheless, the opposition is increasingly structured into the human condition, whether our epoch is aware of it or not. From a pragmatic social constructionist perspective, the lines of opposition are interpreted as historical constructs that give fateful structure to modern life, and their real meaning struggles aborning in our concerted responses. As Simmel (1968: 25) concluded early in this Century, "Although this chronic conflict between form and life has become acute in many historical epochs, none but ours has revealed it so clearly as its basic theme."

# Bibliography

Abbott, Edwin A.
    1983  Flatland. New York: Perennial Library.
Alurista
    1971  Floricanto en Aztlan. Los Angeles: Chicano Studies
          Center, University of California.
Ammerman, Nancy T.
    1987  Bible Believers. New Brunswick: Rutgers University
          Press.
Anderson R.E., and S.G. Wieting
    1976  "Graphical humor and the measurement of attitudi-
          nal ambivalence." Communication Research 3 (3):
          311–326.
Anthony, D., and T. Robbins
    1975  "From symbolic realism to structuralism." Journal
          for the Scientific Study of Religion 14:403–414.
Armstrong, Herbert W.
    1980  The United States and Britain in Prophecy. Pasade-
          na: Worldwide Church of God.
Barber, Bernard
    1983  The Logic and Limits of Trust. New Brunswick: Rut-
          gers University Press.
Bardwick, J.M., and E. Douvan
    1971  "Ambivalence: the socialization of women." Pp.
          147–159 in Vivian Gornick and B.K. Moran (eds.),
          Women in Sexist Society. New York: Basic Books.
Barkun, M.
    1983  "Divided apocalypse." Soundings 65:257–280.

1985 "Nuclear war and millenarian symbols." Paper read at annual meeting of the Society for the Scientific Study of Religion.

Baumeister, Roy
1986 Identity. New York: Oxford University Press.

Becker, Ernest
1975 The Denial of Death. New York: Free Press.

Beckford, James A.
1989 Religion and Advanced Industrial Society. London: Unwin Hyman.

Bellah, Robert N.
1964 "Religious evolution." American Sociological Review 29:358–374.
1968 "The sociology of religion." Pp. 406–414 in David A. Sills (ed.), International Encyclopedia of the Social Sciences, V. 13. New York: Macmillan.
1975 The Broken Covenant. New York: Seabury.
1976 "New religious consciousness and the crisis in modernity." Pp. 333–352 in Charles Y. Glock and Robert N. Bellah (eds.), The New Religious Consciousness. Berkeley: University of California Press.

Bellah, Robert N., Richard Madsen, William M. Sullivan, Ann Swidler, and Steven M. Tipton
1985 Habits of the Heart. Berkeley: University of California Press.

Berger, Peter L.
1963 Invitation to Sociology. Garden City: Anchor Books.
1967 The Sacred Canopy. New York: Doubleday.
1974 "Some second thoughts on the substantive versus functional definitions of religion." Journal for the Scientific Study of Religion 13:125–133.
1980 The Heretical Imperative. New York: Doubleday Anchor.

Berger, Peter L., and Thomas Luckmann
1966 The Social Construction of Reality. Garden City: Doubleday.

Berger, Peter L., Brigitte Berger, and Hansfried Kellner
1973 The Homeless Mind. New York: Random House

Billig, Michael, Susan Condor, Derek Edwards, Mike Gane, David Middleton, and Alan Radley
1988 Ideological Dilemmas. Beverly Hills: Sage Publications.

Blasi, Anthony J., Fabio B. Dasilva, and Andrew J. Weigert
    1978  Toward an Interpretive Sociology. Washington: Uni-
          versity Press of America.

Blumer, Herbert
    1969  Symbolic Interactionism: Perspective and Method.
          Englewood Cliffs: Prentice-Hall.

Boyer, Ernest L.
    1987  College. New York: Harper and Row.

Campbell, Colin
    1987  The Romantic Ethic and the Spirit of Modern Co-
          sumerism. New York: Basil Blackwell.

Candelaria, C.
    1985  "Code switching." Presentation at University of
          Notre Dame Fiesta in honor of Julian Samora.

Chronicle of Higher Education
    1986  "Undergraduates' attitudes on social and economic
          issues." 31:30.

Cohn, W.
    1960  "Social status and the ambivalence hypothesis."
          American Sociological Review 25: 508–513.

Cole, Susan L.
    1985  The Absent One. University Park: The Pennsylvania
          State University Press.

Cooley, Charles H.
    1902/1964  Human Nature and the Social Order. New
          York: Schocken Books.

Coser, Lewis
    1956/1964  The Functions of Social Conflict. New York:
          Free Press.

Coser, Lewis, and Bernard Rosenberg (eds.)
    1976  Sociological Theory, 4th Edition. New York: Macmillan.

Coser, R.L.
    1966  "Role distance, sociological ambivalence, and tran-
          sitional status systems." American Journal of Sociol-
          ogy 72: 173–187.
    1976  "Authority and structural ambivalence in the middle-
          class family." Pp. 566–576 in L.A. Coser and B. Rosen-
          berg (eds.), Sociological Theory. New York: Macmillan.

Davis, F.
    1985  "Clothing and fashion as communication." Pp. 15–27
          in Michael Solomon (ed.), The Psychology of Fash-
          ion. Lexington: Heath.

1987 "Identity ambivalences and fashion: some reflections on the dialectic of the erotic and chaste in dress." Paper delivered at the Annual Meeting of the American Sociological Association. Chicago, IL.

Dench, Geoff
1986 Minorities in an Open Society. New York: Routledge and Kegan Paul.

Denzin, Norman K.
1984 On Understanding Emotion. San Francisco: Jossey-Bass.

Doi, Takeo
1986 The Anatomy of Self. New York: Kodansha International.

Douglas, Mary
1970 Purity and Danger. Baltimore: Penguin Books.
1989 "The background of the grid dimension: a comment." Sociological Analysis 50: 171–176.

Du Bois, W. E. B.
1904 The Souls of Black Folk. Chicago: A. C. McClurg & Co. 4th edition.

Dubos, Rene
1980 The Wooing of the Earth. New York: Charles Scribner's Sons.

Durkheim, Emile, et al.
1964 Essays on Sociology and Philosophy. New York: Harper Torchbook.

Eisenstadt, S.N., and L. Roniger.
1984 Patrons, Clients, and Friends. Cambridge: Cambridge University Press.

Ekman, Paul, and Wallace V. Friesen
1975 Unmasking the Face. Englewood Cliffs: Prentice-Hall.

Elias, Norbert
1939/1982 Power and Civility. New York: Pantheon.

Ellison, Ralph
1953 Invisible Man. New York: Signet.

Erikson, Erik H.
1959 Identity and the Life Cycle: Selected Papers by Erik H. Erikson. Psychological Issues, VI. New York: International Universities Press.

Erikson, Erik H. (ed.)
1978 Adulthood. New York: Norton.

Festinger, Leon
  1957 A Theory of Cognitive Dissonance. Stanford: Stanford University Press.
Finkelstein J.
  1980 "Considerations for a sociology of the emotions." Pp. 111–121 in Norman K. Denzin (ed.), Studies in Symbolic Interaction. Greenwich: JAI Press.
Foote, Nelson N.
  1953 "Love." Psychiatry 16: 245–251.
Franks, David D., and Joseph A. Marolla
  1976 "Efficacious action and social approval as interacting dimensions of self-esteem: a tentative formulation through construct validation." Sociometry 39: 324–341.
Franks, David D. and E. Doyle McCarthy (eds.)
  1989 The Sociology of Emotions. Greenwich: JAI Press.
Frazier, C.E., and T. Meisenhelder
  1985 "Exploratory notes on criminality and emotional ambivalence." Qualitative Sociology 8 (3): 266–284.
Freud, Sigmund
  1913/1964 Totem and Taboo. London: Hogarth.
  1915/1964 Instincts and Their Vicissitudes. London: Hogarth.
  1916–7/1964 The Libido Theory and Narcissism. London: Hogarth.
  1923/1961 The Ego and the Id. London: Hogarth.
  1930/1964 Civilization and Its Discontents. London: Hogarth.
Gecas, Viktor, and Michael Schwalbe
  1983 "Beyond the Looking-Glass Self: social structure and efficacy-based self esteem." Social Psychology Quarterly 46: 77–88.
Geertz, Hildred
  1959 "The vocabulary of emotion." Psychiatry 22: 225–237.
Glock, Charles Y., and Robert N. Bellah (eds.)
  1976 The New Religious Consciousness. Berkeley: University of California Press.
Goffman, Erving
  1959 The Presentation of Self in Everyday Life. Garden City: Doubleday.
  1963 Stigma. Englewood Cliffs: Prentice-Hall.
  1974 Frame Analysis. New York: Harper and Row.
Gordon, S.L.
  1981 "The sociology of sentiments and emotions." Pp.

562–592 in Morris Rosenberg and Ralph H. Turner (eds.), Social Psychology. New York: Basic.

Gouldner, A.W.
1975 "Sociology and the everyday life." Pp. 417–432 in Lewis A. Coser (ed.), The Idea of Social Structure. New York: Harcourt Brace Jovanovich.

Greenspan, S.
1980 "A case of mixed feelings: ambivalence and the logic of emotion." Pp. 223–250 in Amelie O. Rorty (ed.), Explaining Emotions. Berkeley: University of California Press.

Hajda, J.
1968 "Ambivalence and social relations." Sociological Focus 2 (2): 21–28.

Halsell, Grace
1986 Prophecy and Politics. Westport: Lawrence Hill and Co.

Harré, Rom (ed.)
1986 The Social Construction of Emotions. New York: Basil Blackwell.

Heilman, S.C.
1977 "Inner and outer identities: sociological ambivalence among Orthodox Jews." Jewish Social Studies 39: 227–240.

Hewitt, John P. and Peter M. Hall
1973 "Social problems, problematic situations, and quasi-theories." American Sociological Review 38: 367–374.

Hesser, G., and A.J. Weigert
1980 "Comparative dimensions of liturgy: a conceptual framework and feasibility application." Sociological Analysis 41: 215–229.

Hochschild, Arlie R.
1975 "The sociology of feeling and emotion: selected possibilities." Pp. 280–307 in Marcia Millman and Rosabeth M. Kanter (eds.), Another Voice. Garden City: Doubleday Anchor.
1979 "Emotion work, feeling rules and social structure." American Journal of Sociology 35: 551–575.
1983 The Managed Heart. Berkeley: University of California Press.

Hoekema, Anthony A.
1979 The Bible and the Future. Grand Rapids: Eerdmans.

Ichheiser, Gustov
        1970 Appearances and Realities. San Francisco: Jossey-
             Bass.
Inglehart, Ronald
        1990 Culture Shift in Advanced Industrial Societies.
             Princeton: Princeton University Press.
Johnson, D.L., and A.J. Weigert
        1980 "Frames in confession: the social construction of
             sexual sin." Journal for the Scientific Study of Reli-
             gion 19: 368–381.
Jowell, R., S. Witherspoon, and L. Brook
        1986 British Social Attitudes: the 1986 Report. Hants:
             Gower Pubs. Co.
Katz, Irwin
        1981 Stigma. Hillsdale: Earlbaum.
Katz, I., D.C. Glass, D.J. Lucido, and J. Farber
        1977 "Ambivalence, guilt, and denigration of a physically
             handicapped victim." Journal of Personality 45:
             419–429.
Kegan, Robert
        1982 The Evolving Self. Cambridge: Harvard University
             Press.
Kemper, Theodore D.
        1978 A Social Interactional Theory of Emotions. New
             York: John Wiley & Sons.
Keniston, Kenneth
        1968 Young Radicals. New York: Harcourt, Brace, and World.
Klapp, Orrin E.
        1969 Collective Search for Identity. New York: Holt, Rine-
             hart & Winston.
Kurtz, Lester R.
        1986 The Politics of Heresy. Berkeley: University of Cali-
             fornia Press.
LaBarre, Weston
        1972 The Ghost Dance. New York: Delta.
Laing, R.D.
        1971 Self and Others. Baltimore: Pelican Books.
        1972 The Politics of the Family. New York: Vintage.
Langer, Susanne K.
        1942/1958 Philosophy in a New Key. New York: Mentor.
Lasch, Christopher
        1979 The Culture of Narcissism. New York: Norton.

Latané, Bibb and John Darley
1970 The Unresponsive Bystander. New York: Appleton-Century-Crofts.
Lee, Alfred M.
1966 Multivalent Man. New York: Braziller.
Levine, Donald N.
1985 The Flight from Ambiguity. Chicago: The University of Chicago Press.
Lewis, J.D., and A.J. Weigert
1985 "Trust as a social reality." Social Forces 63:967–985.
1985a "Social atomism, holism, and trust." The Sociological Quarterly 26: 455–471.
Lieberman, Jethro K.
1981 The Litigious Society. New York: Basic.
Lifton, Robert J.
1976 The Life of the Self. New York: Simon and Schuster.
1980 The Broken Connection. New York: Touchstone.
1986 The Nazi Doctors. New York: Basic Books.
Lifton, Robert J., and Richard A. Falk
1982 Indefensible Weapons. New York: Basic.
Lindsey, Hal
1977 The Late Great Planet Earth. Grand Rapids: Zondervan.
Luckmann, Thomas
1967 The Invisible Religion. New York: Macmillan.
MacIntyre, Alasdair
1984 After Virtue. Notre Dame: University of Notre Dame Press.
Marris, Peter
1975 Loss and Change. Garden City: Doubleday.
McCarthy, E. Doyle
1989 "Emotions are social things." Pp. 51–72 in David D. Franks and E. Doyle McCarthy (eds.), The Sociology of Emotions. Greenwich: JAI Press.
Mead, George H.
1934 Mind, Self, and Society. Chicago: University of Chicago Press.
Merton, Robert K.
1949/1957 Social Theory and Social Structure. Glencoe: Free Press.
1976 Sociological Ambivalence. New York: Free Press
Merton, Robert K. and E. Barber
1963 "Sociological ambivalence." Pp. 91–120 in E.A.

Tiryakian (ed.), Sociological Theory, Values and Sociological Change. New York: Free Press. Reprinted in R.K. Merton (1976), Sociological Ambivalence. New York: Free Press, pp. 3–31.

Merton, V., R.K. Merton, and E. Barber
1983 "Client ambivalence in professional relationships: the problem of seeking help from strangers." Pp. 13–44 in B.P. DePaulo et al. (eds.), New Directions in Helping. New York: Academic Press.

Milgram, Stanley
1975 Obedience to Authority. New York: Harper Colophon.

Mitroff, I.
1974 "Norms and counternorms in a select group of the Apollo moon scientists: a case study of the ambivalence of scientists." American Sociological Review 39: 579–595.

Mojtabai, A.G.
1986 Blessed Assurance. Boston: Houghton Mifflin.

Morawska, E.
1987 "Sociological ambivalence: the case of East European peasant-immigrant workers in America, 1880s–1930s." Qualitative Sociology 10 (3): 225–250.

Nash, Roderick
1976 Wilderness and the American Mind. New Haven: Yale University Press.

Newman, Katherine S.
1989 Falling from Grace. New York: Vintage Books.

Nye, F.
1976 "Ambivalence in the family." The Family Coordinator 25: 21–31.

O'Connor, James
1987 The Meaning of Crisis. New York: Basil Blackwell.

O'Dea, Thomas F.
1963 "Sociological dilemmas: five paradoxes of institutionalization." Pp. 71–89 in Edward A. Tiryakian (ed.), Sociological Theory, Values, and Sociocultural Change. New York: Harper Torchbook.
1966 The Sociology of Religion. Englewood Cliffs: Prentice-Hall.

Ortega y Gasset, José
1964 What is Philosophy? New York: Norton Library.
1976 On Love. New York: New American Library.

Otto, Rudolf
  1923/1958  The Idea of the Holy. New York: Oxford University Press.
Public Agenda Foundation.
  1984  Voter Options on Nuclear Arms Policy. New York.
Putney, Snell, and Gail J. Putney
  1972  The Adjusted American. New York: Perennial Library, Harper and Row.
Richardson, Laurel
  1985  The New Other Woman. New York: Free Press.
Rieff, Philip
  1966  The Triumph of the Therapeutic. New York: Harper & Row.
Rochberg-Halton, Eugene
  1986  Meaning and Modernity. Chicago: University of Chicago Press.
Room, R.
  1976  "Ambivalence as a sociological explanation: the case of cultural explanations of alcohol problems." American Sociological Review 41: 1047–1065.
Rubin, Lillian B.
  1981  Women of a Certain Age. New York: Harper Colophon.
Scheff, Thomas J.
  1973  "Intersubjectivity and emotion." American Behavioral Scientist 16: 501–511.
  1983  "Toward integration in the social psychology of emotion." Annual Review of Sociology IX: 333–354.
Schell, Jonathan
  1982  The Fate of the Earth. New York: Avon.
Schur, Edwin M.
  1980  The Politics of Deviance. Englewood Cliffs: Prentice-Hall.
Schutz, Alfred
  1962  The Problem of Social Reality. The Hague: Nijhoff.
  1964  Studies in Social Theory. The Hague: Nijhoff.
  1967  The Phenomenology of the Social World. Evanston: Northwestern University Press.
  1970  Reflections on the Problem of Relevance. New Haven: Yale University Press.
Schwartz, Barry
  1986  The Battle For Human Nature. Boston: Norton.
Schwartz, Barry
  1987  George Washington. New York: Free Press.

Seeman, M.
    1953 "Role conflict and ambivalence in leadership."
         American Sociological Review 18: 373–380.
Sennett, Richard
    1978 The Fall of Public Man. New York: Vintage Books.
Sennett, Richard and Jonathan Cobb
    1973 The Hidden Injuries of Class. New York: Vintage Books.
Shapiro, S.A.
    1968 "The ambivalent animal: man in the contemporary
         British and American novel." Centennial Review 12:
         1–22.
Shapiro, Kenneth J.
    1985 Bodily Reflective Modes. Durham: Duke University
         Press.
Shott, S.
    1979 "Emotion and social life: a symbolic interactionist
         analysis." American Journal of Sociology 84: 1317–
         1334.
Simmel, Georg
    1950 The Sociology of Georg Simmel. Edited by Kurt H.
         Wolff. New York: Free Press.
    1968 The Conflict in Modern Culture and Other Essays.
         New York: Teachers College Press.
Slater, Philip E.
    1966 Microcosm. New York: John Wiley and Sons.
Slater, P. and D. Slater
    1965 "Maternal ambivalence and narcissism: a cross-cul-
         tural study." Merrill-Palmer Quarterly 11: 241–259.
Spiegelberg, H.
    1974 "On the right to say 'we': a linguistic and phenomeno-
         logical analysis." Pp. 129– 156 in George Psathas (ed.),
         Phenomenological Sociology. New York: Wiley-Inter-
         science.
Stearns, Carol Z. and Peter N. Stearns
    1986 Anger. Chicago: The University of Chicago Press.
Stone, Gregory P.
    1962 "Appearance and the self." Pp. 86–118 in A.M. Rose
         (ed.), Human Nature and Social Process. Boston:
         Houghton Mifflin.
Stone, Gregory P., and Harvey Farberman
    1981 Social Psychology through Symbolic Interaction.
         New York: Wiley.

Straus, Murray A., Richard J. Gelles, and Suzanne K. Steinmetz
  1980  Behind Closed Doors. New York: Doubleday.
Stryker, Sheldon
  1980  Symbolic Interactionism. Menlo Park: Benjamin/ Cummings.
Swanson, Guy E.
  1967  Religion and Regime. Ann Arbor: University of Michigan Press.
Tavris, Carol
  1982  Anger. New York: Simon and Schuster.
Thom, Gary B.
  1984  The Human Nature of Social Discontent. Totowa: Rowman and Allanheld.
Thomas, Darwin L., Viktor Gecas, Andrew J. Weigert, and Elizabeth A. Rooney
  1974  Family Socialization and Adolescents. Boston: Lexington.
Trilling, Lionel
  1972  Sincerity and Authenticity. Cambridge: Harvard University Press.
Tuan, Yi-Fu
  1974  Topophilia. Englewood Cliffs: Prentice-Hall.
  1979  Landscapes of Fear. Minneapolis: University of Minnesota Press.
Turkle, Sherry
  1984  The Second Self. New York: Simon & Shuster.
Turner, H.L. and J.L. Guth
  1988  "The politics of Armageddon." Paper presented at the Annual Meeting of the Midwest Political Science Association, Chicago, IL.
Turner, Jonathan H. and David Musick
  1985  American Dilemmas. New York: Columbia University Press.
Turner, R.H.
  1976  "The real self: from institution to impulse." American Journal of Sociology 81: 989–1016.
  1978  "The role and the person." American Journal of Sociology 84 : 1–23.
Van Der Leeuw, G.
  1933/1963 Religion in Essence and Manifestation. New York: Harper.

Van Impe, Jack
   1984 America, Israel, Russia, and World War III. Royal
        Oak, MI: Jack Van Impe Ministries.
Vaughan, Peggy
   1989 The Monogamous Myth. New York: Newmarket
        Press.
Wagner-Pacifici, R, and B. Schwartz
   1987 "The Vietnam Veterans Memorial: ambivalence as a
        genre problem." Paper delivered at the Annual
        Meeting of the American Sociological Association,
        Chicago.
Watzlawick, Paul, Janet H. Belvin, and Don D. Jackson
   1967 Pragmatics of Human Communication. New York:
        Norton.
Weart, Spencer R.
   1988 Nuclear Fear. Cambridge: Harvard University Press.
Weber, Max
   1958 The Protestant Ethic and the Spirit of Capitalism.
        New York: Scribners.
Weigert, Andrew J.
   1983 Social Psychology. Notre Dame: University of Notre
        Dame Press.
   1988 "Christian eschatological identities and the nuclear
        context." Journal for the Scientific Study of Religion
        27: 175–191.
Weigert, A.J., and R. Hastings
   1977 "Identity loss, family, and social change." American
        Journal of Sociology 82: 1171–1185.
Weigert, Andrew J., and E. Sughrue
   1988 "The Button: A Meadian ethical reflection on the
        nuclear situation." Paper delivered at the annual
        meeting of the Midwest Sociological Society.
Weigert, A.J., J.S. Teitge, and D. Teitge
   1986 Society and identity. New York: Cambridge Universi-
        ty Press.
Wexler, Philip
   1983 Critical Social Psychology. London: Routledge &
        Kegan Paul.
Wheelwright, Phillip
   1968 Metaphor and Reality. Bloomington: Indiana Univer-
        sity Press.

White, Geoffrey M. and John Kirkpatrick (eds.)
    1985  Person, Self, and Experience. Berkeley: University of
          California Press.
White, Robert W.
    1965  "The experience of efficacy in schizophrenia." Psy-
          chiatry 28: 199–211.
Williams, Christine L.
    1989  Gender Differences at Work. Berkeley: University of
          California Press.
Williams, N.W., G. Sjoberg, and A.F. Sjoberg
    1980  "The bureacratic personality: an alternative view."
          The Journal of Applied Behavioral Science 16:
          389–405.
Wiseman, Jacqueline P. (ed.)
    1976  The Social Psychology of Sex. New York: Harper.
Wolfe, Alan
    1989  Whose Keeper? Berkeley: University of California
          Press.
Wuthnow, Robert
    1988  Meaning and Moral order. Berkeley: University of
          California Press.
    1988a The Restructuring of American Religion. Princeton:
          Princeton University Press.
Yankelovich, Daniel
    1982  New Rules. New York: Random House.
Yankelovich, D. and J. Doble
    1984  "The public mood: nuclear weapons and the U.S.S.R."
          Foreign Affairs 63: 33–46.
Yinger, J. Milton
    1982  Countercultures. New York: Free Press.
Young, Michael
    1988  The Metronomic Society. Cambridge: Harvard Uni-
          versity Press.
Zborowski, Mark
    1969  People in Pain. San Francisco: Jossey-Bass.
Zielyk, I.V.
    1966  "On ambiguity and ambivalence." Pacific Sociologi-
          cal Review 9: 57–64.
Zijderveld, Anton C.
    1979  On Cliches. Boston: Routledge and Kegan Paul.
Zurcher, Louis A.
    1977  The Mutable Self. Beverly Hills, CA: Sage.

# Index